My Ancestor's Path Is My Future Journey

MY ANCESTOR'S PATH IS MY FUTURE JOURNEY

Stephanie Colligan-Ishola

ARPress
ILLUMINATING IDEAS
EMPOWERING VOICES

ARPress
45 Dan Road Suite 5
Canton MA 02021
Hotline: 1(888) 821-0229
Fax: 1(508) 545-7580

Ordering Information:

Quantity sales. Special discounts are available on quantity purchases by corporations, associations, and others. For details, contact the publisher at the address above.

Printed in the United States of America.

ISBN-13:   Softcover   979-8-89356-502-7

             eBook   979-8-89356-503-4

Library of Congress Control Number: 2024902544

Memoirs of a Council member of the Atakapa Ishak Nation

My journey began from the footsteps of my ancestors' path. In fact, the historical timeline started from the region of Africa Cameroon/ Congo/Benin/Mali/Nigeria/Ivory Coast/Ghana tracing the regions of Senegal/ Southeastern Bantu/South Central Hunters-Gathers/North Africa/Asia South/Europe Iberian Peninsula/Scandinavia/Ireland/ Europe West/East, until they migrated to the shores of North America, encompassing the entire lands of the Americas.

Acknowledgments

I would like to thank Jean M. Auel, author of *The Plains of Passage* (Earth's Children series), for inspiring me that day many years ago, when we first met at her book release in Texas. I was fortunate to attend with my supervisor from the Texas Art Supply, where I worked and enjoyed helping local artists and developed my craft.

Also, during my eight-week stay in Louisiana, I was able to conduct some research in my native home known by most family members "Le Petit Paris."

Special thanks to my uncle, for giving me a place to stay while I completed my research for my manuscript. Love you, Uncle Mike and Aunt Jackie, for opening your door to me with welcoming arms we Louisianians are best known for, among other specialties.

To the employees at St. Landry Parish Tax Assessor, Henry Fountanire, and Iesha Gabriel for being patient with me with my thousands of questions and unannounced meetings. I appreciate the "Southern hospitality" you both provided me throughout my research at the courthouse.

To Gene Thibodeaux, distant family member and author of the historical reference book *On the Banks of Plaquemine Brulée*, who sent me in spirit kind words of encouragement to continue my dream to become a storyteller.

To my baby sister, Dionne Colligan, who helped me with some of my note-taking during our trips to several surrounding parishes.

Also, deep sincere gratitude to my cousin, the family historian, Eva Colligan Iford, for gathering some special mementos of our family's legacy and passing down the baton to me.

Finally, my love goes out to my children and their father for supporting me in turning my life experiences and visions into print, for the whole world to view.

And to all the others who gave their time and participated in interviews to further the progress of my research.

Special thanks to my great-uncle, Chief Michael Amos, former chief of the Atakapa-Ishak Nation. I know from affirmation from the Great Spirit I would know exactly what to do, as he stated to me during our intense communication.

CHIEF MICHAEL AMOS

This book is dedicated to the
memory of my father,
Paul Isaac Colligan Sr., and ancestors

1937–1998

This book is intended to tell the story, both in words and pictures, by enabling my audience to envision my journey and ancestors' path unfolding through my very own eyes, supported by genealogy research, interviews, and my dream visions. Take a journey with me and them down the path to spiritual freedom! This was rehearsed and written for seventeen years by the little girl, Anajatjaguar, who was gifted with keen sight, like the beautiful but noble and loyal jaguar, my spirit animal. In addition, my book is intended to restore the soul. In all of the essence of life, people must continue to believe in a higher calling to obtain inner peace with harmonious love for creation and all inhabitants in our society. I was reared to have faith in the Creator and remember my family values. First, worship, and second, give charity, which begins at home. But equally important is the nurturing, loving, and caring environment where you are taught you can be all that you can. I descended from a clan that communicated openly, expressing one's feelings while having the ability to be honest and maintain self-respect and respect for others while upholding integrity, even when your opinion may differ among family and society. My upbringing allowed me to be understanding of others through empathy and not be judgmental. Growing up in a diverse culture presents opportunities for one to adapt to different life experiences quite different from a nuclear family. Despite the many trial and tribulations in my life growing up, I persevered to become a self-sufficient individual, who did not give up on her dreams and aspirations to achieve her goals. My motto is "Try and try until you fulfill your life dreams." Trial and effort define courage, and courage takes practice to beat the odds! This is testimonial truth from my life experiences. Continue to be a light in the darkness and be obedient to God and practice what you believe in. My earthly father who I loved dearly and who will always have a place in my heart was a true warrior and comforter in this world. He was my role model and touched the hearts of many, but was unable to quench the ache that was lingering in him. The enemy is always present and tries to keep most of us from our heritage and birth right on Mother Earth. The obedient ones are faced with many obstacles on the path to discovering their true destiny. Without our original map, how are we to know where we are going or where we have descended from, when we have been born cut off from the tree of life and given a false image in its place for hope. We must ask ourselves this question: Do we know why we are put here on this earth? Without a doubt the Almighty Creator is all knowing and in control of all affairs on this earth and most definitely the hereafter. Even our existence is preordained, when and where it will manifest, and we shall begin being spiritually connected to our Creator, then the beginning of an individual path and the great quest for the true essence of life will begin. For a fact, it is written, My people will die from lack of knowledge.

Knowledge is power, and we must follow the teachings of our ancestors and great leaders that have died for us to be free of mental bondage. The truth and the way is written in the stars! First step to achieving inner peace and salvation is to have a one-on-one relationship with the Creator. This submission breathes forth a humility of self, which is the key to the building blocks or termed "foundation" to love, peace, and self-awareness on this earth, through an awakening of true self, and is achieved through fasting, praying, and purifying ourselves. I'm thankful that I began to seek and my Heavenly Father answered. I'm truly blessed and have always heard the word but not really understanding its true meaning. When my dad was dying, my eyes began to truly open and search for answers to why we are born and then we must die. Well, I became confused and began my test. I remember one night in the fall of 1993, I almost died and was in a coma for five days, because of medical negligence with a fever of over 105 degrees and had infection throughout my blood stream. My Creator had a guardian angel on standby in the emergency room, who began to care for me. She was a non-Western doctor who believed in holistic treatment, and within hours, my fever broke and vital signs were stabilized and all signs of life returned to my body. After a week, I was visited by the physician, and she stated to me, "You were very critical, and the other ER physician had given up on you, but God did not and said you have more work on this earth." From that moment,

I knew within myself I must follow God's commandments. My near-death experience happened for a reason, and shortly after, I met my soul mate, a foreigner from Africa, and was captured by his personality. We talked for hours until the sunrise, and we knew that we were meant for each other, or we thought so. We decided to start a life together not focused on our beliefs and faith. We just did not think it should affect our relationship, but time would tell. I was excited and felt my dreams had come true since, I transitioned into adulthood, I prayed that I would one day have a spouse with similar characteristics like my father. I decided to introduce him to my immediate family and extended family members. The comments that I received were negative and stereotyping of people born in Africa. We decided to share our lives together, and he helped me to live a healthier lifestyle by eliminating pork, red meats, and processed foods. These foods take a long time to digest and break down by the digestive system. I have been suffering from chronic illnesses and allergies throughout my adolescent age. My immune system would produce rashes all over my body as a defense mechanism for the bad lifestyle and diet I had, and so did many of my family members, including my father and siblings. I knew deep down in my heart the physical ailments were associated with my cultural environment and not so much as hereditary as many physicians would attest to. So the little girl lost and disconnected from her heritage and ancestry began to rely on him, and he shared knowledge and wisdom through natural African remedies for healing. He had knowledge of the different herbs and would go to the market to buy the roots for his mother to help others in need. She was a true believer of the Almighty and a healer to man. I began to drink concoctions and brews that were very bitter on my pallet but produced an effect of cleansing making me feel better within a couple of hours. I was sold into a new lifestyle change that rejuvenated the inner self to promote a sense of well-being of mind, body, and spirit. This period of transition in my life involved enlightenment through purification, fasting, and prayer. I began to have dreams and visions like I had when I was a young child. In fact, to be specific, I was born with a veil, being able to see the past, present, and future.

My mother avoids talking about my birth. She only remembers it was a complicated pregnancy and she cannot recall the hour I was born.

Neither was the time recorded on my birth certificate. It is a mystery, just like many unexplained phenomena surrounding my birth. I was born on tribal land in the Atakapa region at Lafayette Charity Hospital Historical Louisiana, which is a hospital servicing Native American families built on Atakapa land.

Copy of my birth certificate in Lafayette, Louisiana.

This document proves the validity of my baptism performed under Christ the King Mission in Grand Coteau, Louisiana, now called St. John Berchman Catholic Church, where Native people could not attend services with whites in the early '60s because of Jim Crow laws, where the Jesuit Priest came to North America during the seventeenth century to preach among the Indians. Pope Francis was a former priest of the Jesuit priesthood established by St. Ignatius.

During the time of my birth in 1962, my father was a farmer on his grandfather's land that was transferred to his father, John Colligan, back in 1959. In the document below, my grandfather assigned to his heir's mineral rights. I've yet to see any royalties that my father inherited from his father. In fact, it was rumored that my granddad was forced out of his property by ruthless men.

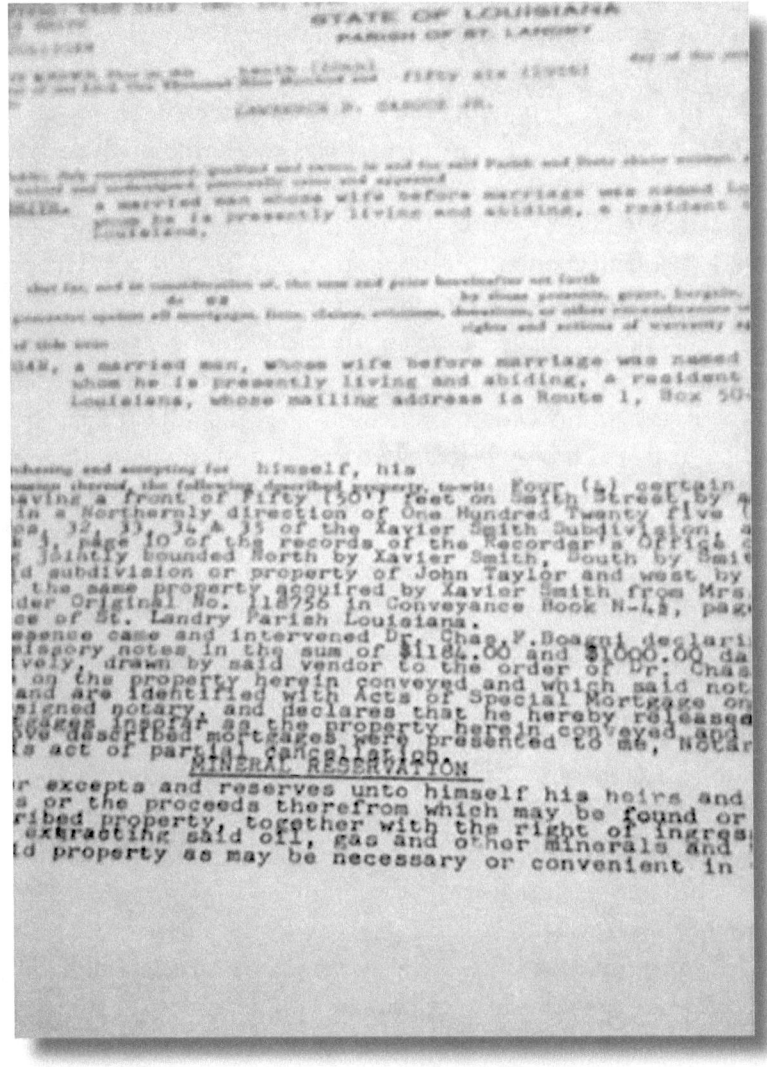

Consequently, being born in the era of the '60s presented a lot of hardships and struggles for my family who were five generations of farmers. They made a living by cultivating land for their self-sufficiency to survive with limited resources similar to their ancestors seventy years ago. Furthermore, I grew up in a multiracial and multicultural background. My grandparents from my father's side are of Irish, German, French, Spanish, Native American, and African descent, similar to my mother's side, but her mother's male lineage migrated from the Iberian Peninsula, France, and Africa as well. Having such a diverse ethnicity allowed for many of my family members to be classified as Creole, Mexican, Caucasian, and Mulatto earlier in the decades when they were former immigrants from various countries. In the early 1700s, Louisiana was a lucrative investment to attract and monopolize during the colonial period. The Louisiana Purchase involved 828, 000 square miles of U.S. territory. It was the home of Paleo Indians from my ancestral lineage over thousands of years ago. This time was marked and would be written throughout history as the melting pot of diversity on all economic levels, known as "The Who's Who and the Have Nots," perhaps a matter of opinion to some people in the South. Truly, Louisiana is a majestic haven where the lands are vast. Grain and cattle was plenty to all and every living creature that thrive. Many of the first settlers of my pedigree were well-known families and bearers of royal crests from faraway places, with wealth and privilege. In fact, my DNA results mentioned earlier in the preface that our bloodlines are of the universal rainbow. Many of our descendants today, acquired these characteristic traits and behaviors through biological and genealogical predisposition of my ancestors mentioned below.

First, early history notes the Carriere, Charlot, Miller, and Colligan lineage arrived during the Great Migration, settling in the United States in the seventeenth century. One of my ancestors, Louis Carriere, arrived in Mobile, Alabama in 1764. There are many contemporary notables who bear the name Carriere. Secondly, my fourth great-grandfather, Jacque Charlot arrived in Louisiana around the 1700's. Thirdly, the Miller surname is thought to have originated in Bavaria, Germany. Thousands of German settlers came to North America between the mid- seventeenth century and the twentieth centuries. The hardships of the long voyage were balanced by the opportunity to escape poverty and religious persecution. "Many of these descendants of these settlers still populate the states of Pennsylvania, Texas, New York, Illinois, and California, while some migrated to South Carolina, known as the Millers' Cherokee connection."

According to reservation rolls, some of my ancestors from the Cherokee tribe migrated from the American Southwest to the Great Lakes region. Lastly, the Colligan family were very powerful Gaelic chiefs until eighteenth century. The original surname O'Cochlains became known as Colligan to make registration of the name easier. It is documented that one of my ancestor, Bernard Colligan was a wealthy planter in Opelousas, Louisiana. In 1859 Adeline (Matilda) Brown, my third great-grandmother, was a slave on a ship named the *Jefferson*, who arrived in New Orleans, and was employed by Bernard Colligan.

During Adeline's employment, she was impregnated by her master and gave birth to my great-grandfather, Sylvester "Red Bud." Former family historian said that Red Bud went to live with the Venable family. Even today, the Venable children acknowledge Bud and his descendants as cousins.

According to the 1900s census, Adeline Brown was living on land she acquired in Police Jury Ward 2, St. Landry. One of my elderly uncles shared that when his great-grandmother had his grandfather, "Red Bud," it was rumored that the Colligan's kept the red-haired baby boy with blue eyes while the mother's whereabouts were unknown. My extensive research revealed that Adeline Brown never left St. Landry Parish. She has remained there until the ripe old age of ninety-five. It has been the talk of the town in Louisiana for decades that my family clan ran the town and many surrounding parishes where they were landowners. Some acquired their land through land grants with the Spanish government and others because of the service, where most of the Native American and other minorities have helped to defend America.

My great-grandfather, being the son of a privileged Irish planter, purchased large amounts of land in Coulee Croche, known as Cankton, Louisiana, where family members still reside today. The "conveyances" reveal over 2600 acres of land transferred to Sylvester Colligan, in the state of Louisiana. I researched plat books and deeds at the Opelousas

Courthouse, showing that he owned several plantations, and found that he hired someone to refurbish the buildings, in addition to land from the Southwestern Louisiana Co. and Railroad Co. (Southwestern La Lastro Leo), of St. Landry Parish in January 25, 1887. Sylvester Colligan purchased and accepted for himself and his heirs, and assigned and acknowledged delivery and possession of the parcel of land.

I've heard stories about my father spending time with his cousins on the Banks of Plaquemine Brulée, where Red Bud drove the range with his sons from the marriage of Eva Charlot, daughter of Don Louis Charlot and Alexandrine Chretien, parents classified as "colored Indians." Back when I did some of my research at the

Acadia Library in Cankton, I received a copy of *On the Banks of Plaquemine Brulée*, written by Gene Thibodeaux. I was delighted to meet his wife and receive a book about the life experiences of my great-grandfather and the place where other family members called home. According to Gene Thibodeaux, "The exciting history of the town of "Plaquemine" revolves around the land and how to make a living from it. The Atakapas Indians hunted and fished within the prairies, woodlands and streams"

I decided to visit the cemetery in Cankton where my great-grandfather is buried, along with his uncle, John T. Colligan, a former Confederate soldier, in the white cemetery. In the late 1800s, there was a significant difference of burial procedures among social classes. Furthermore, many slaves were not afforded the comfort of their white counterparts, and many were buried with no headstones or plaques for distinguishing one from another. This serves as an example of racial discrimination. During this tumultuous period, yellow fever ravaged the Deep South, and many slaves' birth and burials records were forgotten and erased, never to see the light of day.

My great-grandfather, Sylvester "Red Bud"
Colligan, and Eva Charlot Colligan (wife).

Bud married Eva Charlot. This marks the beginning of the Colligan-
Charlot union. They had seven sons and one daughter. One of the male
children of Sylvester and Eva was the late John Joseph Colligan, my
grandfather, pictured below with his wife, Emma Miller Colligan.

My grandparents, the late Mr. and Mrs. John Colligan Sr.

A true cowboy and one of the best poker player who always entertained his friends after a long, drawn-out game. He would cheer the souls of many with a tune from his accordion.

My aunt Yvonne, whom I never knew but seen a little girl who resembled her through one of my visions before writing my book in 2013.

My father, Paul Isaac Colligan Sr., and mother,
Emma Miller Colligan, were Creole mulattos. Picture
taken in the late '40s in Cankton, Louisiana.

My grandmother, Emma, was the firstborn daughter of Edmond
Miller and Sophie Wheeler Miller. I had much in common with my
grandmother. My maternal grandfather Henry "King" Pierre III was
renting land as a sharecropper to farm and provide for his family. I
experienced firsthand what it felt like to work in a field as a youth.
Even though my father relocated his immediate family to Texas, along
with other family members, we would travel back and forth as seasonal
farm workers in the summer to assist my grandfather with the usual
farm chores to sustain the family. This period in the early '60s was fun
and also sad at times because it was an era of injustice and cruelty to
descendants of farmers and sharecroppers in the South. I reminisce on
the happy memories of being a child surrounded by large groups of

family. It was a lesson to remember God and support your kin. I recall visiting family members who decided to be classified as another race to receive better economic opportunities. My dad would go to see his family openly in towns classified as "white" parishes. He waited until sunset to avoid bringing his little "tinted skin children" he so loved but was looked upon as too black. The color of one's skin played an important role in Louisiana for decades. Many parishes in Louisiana were designed to segregate the Indian families to feel inferior to one another by intermingling for purpose of economic growth. Some family members bought into the new idea for status and improved living. However, the consequences were horrific, when Caucasian men would take advantage of women of color.

Many women would have to abandon their babies to families and orphanages to continue the facade or be outcast by the men who abused them. In other cases, many women would rely on the parish priest to wage their wars for them by baptizing their babies with the white man's name or other ethnic surnames. To be exact, there were a lot of unwed mothers and mistresses of prominent men in the state of Louisiana whose names were given to their illegitimate offspring. Nevertheless, these free-born inhabitants are what we know as Creole, Mulattos, Quadroons, Octoroons, and Negro.

According to the 1850 census, it showed that some Indian households were enumerated. Indians who were not taxed were not enumerated; simple terms meaning not recorded or listed on any government records. However, the categories changed a bit that year. The families of Indians who renounced their tribal rights under state or territorial laws became citizens. In such cases the censor taker would write "Ind" by the names to identify their racial ethnicity. In 1860 many Indian families acculturated into the white man's world and began dressing and mingling among them on different social levels. For example, my matriarch, Adeline Brown, during her service to the Colligan family, resulted in birthing a biracial child my great-grandfather, Sylvester Colligan. Much propaganda had spread surrounding the whereabouts of Adeline Brown and the child. It was no secret that Sylvester's father relocated with the child after the death of his wife to live with relatives. It was very easy for Red Bud's father to keep his son. His skin was white as snow, eyes blue as shining zircon, red hair like the bud of an Irish rose, and was nicknamed Red Bud. My great-grandfather and his sons were cattlemen who rode horses for miles and did farming as well. He was very business savvy despite being uneducated, but his name gave him much prestige and opportunities to purchase and transfer property deeds to many other Native families throughout the St. Landry Parish. While researching in the historic vaults in the county courthouse, I ran across a land deed dated October 27, 1975 showing the land he acquired stretched from Zick Miller Road to Wild Rose Road of what is now called Cankton.

I recall my cousin Eva telling me a story about her father who worked for the Sibille family running the cotton gin and fixing roads. My Great uncle, found a barrel of money buried in the ground on the old dirt road where he was laying down gravel. He turned in the money to Gustave Sibille, according to cousin Eva. One thing is certain, the

Colligan's were honest and lived up to their family crest with pride. According to a narrative by Robert Sibille, it mentions he bought property from my great-grandfather, Sylvester Bud Colligan, referred to as a former slave. I would disagree with my ancestor being referred to as a slave because he had massive wealth and owned many acres of land throughout several parishes.

My great-grandmother, Sophie Wheeler Miller (1881–1977), Emma Miller Colligan (daughter). Sophie was the daughter of

Benjamin Franklin Wheeler (circa 1840–1919) and Julie Beverly Wheeler (1860–1915), daughter of Isaac Beverly and Sophy Minix, who were referred to as "The Forgotten Jews. Sophie Wheeler Miller was a strong and courageous woman who would not be broken by the hierarchy of Catholicism that was practiced among the South. Many priests would perform services in Latin, a tongue that many Native people did not understand to exercise control over the masses. I recall a personal interview with Miss Bonnie Rose, who stated, "Your great-grandmother was an outspoken person with wisdom and said to many families and friends, if we cannot understand the language or able to speak it when the priest are facing the opposite direction to the congregation, then how will we know if we are worshipping God?" She left the Catholic faith and joined a Baptist church called Mt. Zion, where she was married to my great-grandfather, Edmond Miller, by Rev. C.S. Malbrue (minister of the gospel).

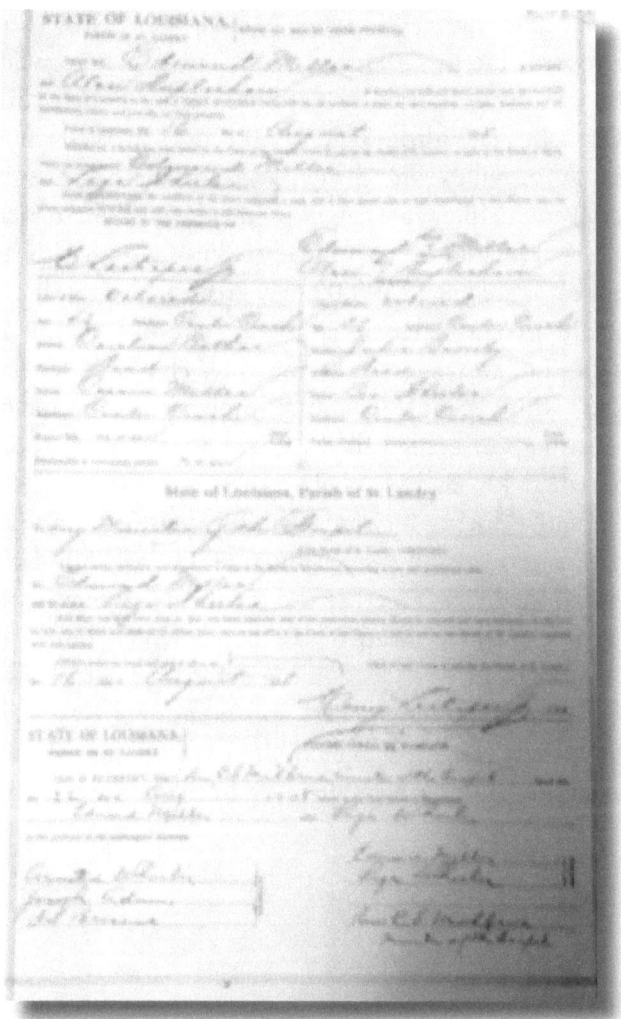

Here is a copy of their marriage license showing
the distinct classification of Native Americans
during this period known also as "colored."

Reflecting back, where have my Miller Familia not lived? Living in Virginia, North and South Carolinas, Arkansas, Mississippi, Alabama, Georgia, Texas, and Louisiana. Especially significant places like Cameron, Bienville, Cow Island, Coulee Crouche, Vermillion, Terrebonne, Bayou Beouf, Grand Chenier, and Grand Coteau. Even today as we speak, one can see the Miller name all over the cities and towns on signs and landmarks throughout the U.S.

My great-grandfather, Cesaire Miller, was listed on his son's marriage record. He was a known as a Civil War hero who fought in 1861–1865 and was married to Caroline Bathus Barker and resided in Coulee Crouche, according to an 1860 census in Western Vermillion, Louisiana, Abbeyville, where my great-grandfather was living with his father, Peter Miller, a farmer in the Vermillion parish with his wife, Amelia. His estate was valued at $500 along with all personal belongings estimated at $1500.00. My great-great-grandfather's family were documented as "free inhabitants" enumerated by the federal government. He was age six at the time. He and his family were classified as" white" people by choice, preferably to escape persecution and mistreatment of being called Indian. So, the story goes they lived away from their kin to hide their true identity to not feel shame or embarrassment. Moving forward, the U.S. census did not specify how to record Indian or mixed races. Subsequently in 1880, my family had three generations living together the identical way many of them live today. For instance, the head of the house would be the father. My families' occupations were predominately in agriculture after the war, and their wives were homemakers and occasionally assisted in doing chores around the farm. Older children would contribute, with the exception of the family elder remaining in the home due to old age.

Caroline Barker was the mother of my great-grandfather, Edmond Miller. She was the daughter of Harrison Barker. I had a dream once in 2012 that I was accompanying her on a Greyhound bus to relocate to Arkansas to meet family members. On the trip she told me, "You have Indian ancestry. Look and me and look at yourself." The bus stopped and she got off and went into a makeshift barber shop with red sand blowing in the wind.

Cora Savoie Malbrough is the daughter of Ernest Savoie.

My great-aunt, Cora, age 105, lived in Cankton, Louisiana, where there are several oil rigs producing crude oil. She said to me, "Life was hard. I was born on a farm in the wilderness and was farming and you don't have much and I asked the lord to lengthen my days and the days be lengthened by years. And I continued to pray that he sends me people I have not seen. Because my heart is carrying the body and the body is weak."

Camilia Harmon married Ernest Savoie, son of
Caroline Barker. My ancestors have sustained their
livelihood through agriculture for centuries.

"In 1890 census takers would manipulate records for Indian people
with a trace of back blood to be listed as African. Things changed
dramatically between 1920 and 1930 for Indians. Many were made
American citizens. Before 1924, Indians who lived on reservations
were considered to be citizens of their tribe and not American citizens.
However, the period echoes the 1830s lawsuits about Sovereign Tribal
rights." Moreover, Indians living on a reservation were people missing
from the census prior to 1930. My grandmother, Emma Miller, and
her father, Edmond Miller, in the 1930 census Jury Ward 2, St. Landry,
Louisiana were classified as multiracial. Many families passed off as
white with other families during the late 1890s. My great-grandfather,
Edmond Miller, lived with his mother and father and other extended
family members.

Many of my direct descendants listed on Dawes application rolls were blended with explores and traders from England, Scotland, Ireland, and Germany. The Francis men were of both Portuguese and Spanish descent. The Francis males inherited hazel eyes and unique features that still serves as a dominant trait in the male descendants of today. My mother's great grandfather Eduardo Francis married Francois Broussard and lived in St. Martinville, Louisiana, in the Atakapa district.

From this union, they had my great-grandfather, Edwin Francis who wedded Rosaline Francis and had my grandmother Mabel Francis. She married Henry "King" Pierre, the son of Mia Johnson and Henry Pierre Sr., who died during World War I. Henry Pierre Jr., courted and married Mabel Francis. They were farmers all their lives, with a strong work ethic. Together they provided for their family through endurance, perseverance, and love. Their belief system was built on putting God first and sending their children to church and school. Even when times were hard, they were a peaceful and respected family by all in the town.

Pictured are my grandparents, Henry Pierre
Jr. and Mabel Francis Pierre.

The Pierre clan has been a prominent family since the matriarch, Marie Pierre, was the wife of the chief of the Chitimacha tribe. Today, many of the families still reside in Lafayette, Youngsville, Breaux Bridge, Charenton, Louisiana, Texas, and Mississippi, from earlier migration in Virginia and Washington.

My uncle, Michael Pierre, would whisper to me quite often that his father told him, "We are Blackfoot Indians." In fact, he said, "You must not tell a soul because in Morgan City, the people say the white men are killing Indians." I just laughed and went my way until a relative twenty years later mentioned a family member built a shrine in her home to pay homage to the Blackfoot ancestors. Nevertheless, my uncle has never told me anything that was untrue. He has a healing hand with the gift of relieving pain from parts of the body through acupressure. He developed this gift from my grandfather. He is a skilled laborer by trade. It's very interesting how his hands can offer healing just like his dad did for many decades earlier. I too found myself having similar gifts.

After Spending eight weeks in Africa, I decided to campaign for health and wellness, my first order of business, as I chose to call the great plan involved self-redemption. Nigeria was a liberating experience and I enjoyed spending time with my second family. I went sightseeing and tasted cuisines like pepper soup, amala, and plantain (typical Yoruba dishes). I recall my first night as we gathered around the dining table being served. I looked at my plate with a perplexed look. My response was, "Why am I receiving three pieces of meat fit for a small child?" Then the response I got was, "It takes time for a large portion of meat to digest in the system." I did not want to hear this because I was accustomed to eating a six-or eight-inch steak almost every other day of my life. I learned a new way of life and began adjusting to a healthier way of living. I realized that I began feeling better and was not plagued with my regular allergies. My skin began to totally transform, and my body weight decreased within a couple of days. I ate only natural whole foods with no additives or chemicals. Processed food was a part of my past. I also enjoyed evening strolls up and down the hilltop of Ibadan, where my children's second great-grandfather ruled (Oba). In fact, the statue is casted in bronze for all onlookers. I was elated to confirm that my children have a royal bloodline. Overall, my focus was to learn about the native medicinal herbs from the motherland. My mother-in-law prepared teas and blood roots to purify the blood from all parasitic activity that has wreaked havoc within my body. In my heart, I prayed to the Creator to rid me of a generation of practices of eating pork that is forbidden by man in the Holy Book. Well, it was a challenging time to maintain continuity, but I was blessed to succeed. I was thirty pounds lighter, had a natural tan, and returned back to America with simple remedies costing less than a few dollars, that were extremely effective. I decided to open an African store to help people who were interested in learning about African culture. I had just returned from a spiritual journey involving the healing of the "whole body." It was confirmed during a spiritual prayer involving many elders (sheik) arranged by my mother-in-law. Once I returned back home to my normal daily activity, I was on a mission to help others through fasting, prayer, and living a better life. I have had death premonitions of many people who have died shortly after encountering the individual. The strange thing about these death premonitions is that they come true, and after being in a dream state, these people ask me to pray for them. It was revealed to me later on in my life why I was chosen to help others. Seems kind of strange to hear but life is full of unexplainable sightings and personal experiences. I'm an individual who can see things from the past, present, and future. In the South, the saying is that when things happened like this, it's because the person is lucky. Being born with a veil is very rare. In fact, History states that only a few notable people like Emperor Charlemagne, Sigmund Freud, Napoleon, and the actress Lillian Gish have this gift. I know from personal experience that many family and friends have spoken with me during their last days, hours, and minutes of life, confirmed my gift. All these individuals requested for me to pray for them. I find myself following in the footsteps of some of my ancestors who were Indian shamans. Both of my grandfathers from both my father and mother's side would help people with chronic ailments. I've witnessed many people looking for them to assist them with their health dilemmas. I believe it is why I've been destined to help others in any way. I contribute most of my knowledge of medicinal remedies from my trip to Africa and divine intervention. I helped a coworker to achieve a healthy lifestyle with African roots and instructions to follow for six weeks, the exact time new cells regenerate in the body. I've seen images of the physical body with all its organs and its functions. One of my coworkers was diagnosed with ovarian cancer. She asked if I would assist her with a lifestyle change. I agreed and said I would prepare the root (tea) to take along with her. We prayed together during our break time, and she informed me that she was going to retake her test. Her results were negative. She was excited and told me she had a dream about me in a white dress and barefooted in a forest with leaves in my hand, with a large white plane over my head following me. Later that evening, she asked her father to speak with me over the phone. He told me, "Thanks for helping my daughter." I supported a lot of coworkers with their lifestyle changes.

Various herbs, e.g., rosehips, lemon peel, milk thistle, blood root, stomach root, sage, etc.

Most of these herbs are known to boost the immune and nervous system, first, by reducing high blood pressure, like the herb garlic and a host of other known remedies.

I've taken these remedies for over twenty years and have seen improvements with my overall health. Some of my family members called me a witch and refused to try natural remedies until many years after I continued to take these remedies developing a stronger immune system. In addition, the natural remedies are proven beneficial to repair damaged cells and rejuvenate aging cells. I enjoy using a natural cream developed by my spouse Wasiu Ishola, and sold in African Heritage Gallery located in Houston, Texas. I continued to do community service and help women and teens in crisis. I consider myself a humanitarian and have watched my parents and extend family members care for others. My mother taught religious classes for over thirty years. She volunteers her time to the youth and her congregation. I have continued my service to help my fellow man since my adolescent years. The experience of traveling to Africa filled a void that would be explored on a grand scale. I created a black history program to educate teens from a diverse background about African culture and the blending of its culture in America.

My ancestors traveled thousands of years ago during the Old Stone Age, also called Paleolithic Period. I discovered the true reason for my visions, which is to inform the masses that my ancestors still live through me. I have seen chiefs from my ancestral lineage in my visions informing me about my position to guiding our people to the right path. I remember when I was a young teenager, my family wanted me to be a nun. I did not want to devote my life with the restrictions of not having a family. I knew I could still help people throughout my life without becoming a nun. Many nights in my dreams, I was seeing deceased people forming a line and me being called to help them cross over from the earthly plane. It scared me often because I thought I was going to die. So I would pray, hoping to not see dead people in my dreams. Every encounter I had with them was "Please pray for us" and "Help us get to the light." I've seen people that were deceased family members that I've never met before because they were old ancestors from both sides of my family. While, conducting my research in 2013, I visited family elders to learn more about our heritage. In the beginning, I never intended on writing a book about my life. I had enough crisis throughout my lifetime that kept me puzzled about my true destiny. Until one night after the birth of my second son, I decided to begin reading the Holy Qur'an. I had always been around people from the Nation of Islam and others who practice different religions.

I had my reservations about Islam, but I'm not going to elaborate or debate on various religious belief systems. The sole purpose of worship is to pray to only the Creator and associate no other with him. I prayed to learn the opening prayer in the Holy Qur'an. I wanted to learn how to speak it because my younger daughter was attending an Islamic school, and I had attended one of her programs and listened to her recite Arabic. It brought chills and tears to my eyes. I felt a sense of peace and unimaginable joy.

I went to sleep that night, and I saw a man with a turban on his head and long robe standing on a prayer rug. Then we were elevated up into the sky. I heard the recitation of the prayer, "Al Faitha." I was instructed to recite along with the man. There were words written in light, and I did as I was instructed. Then immediately after awakening I began reciting the prayer in Arabic just as I was taught in the dream by the man. I could not believe it! It was a miracle from my Creator. I told my husband what happened, and he explained that "mala'ika" taught me the prayer in my dream. This affirmation was solely the driving force for me to take my "Shahada," saying *"La ilaha illa Allah wa-Muhammad rasul Allah"*. meaning "God is one and the Prophet Muhammad is his messenger." I remembered one of my dreams that occurred in the month of October 1999, shortly after my father's death, that I was visiting an old large plantation house with my young daughter and someone was looking for us. Afterwards, I overheard a man dressed in black instructing someone to go inside my room. The man stated, "That is where she hid the baby girl." So I took my daughter and hid her, and a woman entered and said, "There she is." So I grabbed my daughter and ran outside and two men began chasing me. I saw an elder woman sitting in a rocking chair on the yard and she just stared at me. I ran across the yard and climbed over a high fence with my daughter without looking behind. I entered a busy highway, trying to get a ride, but people kept driving past me. I began proceeding down a narrow road. Then a man approached me and stated, "I'll help you," and when I looked at his face, it changed to a distorted evil figure. Also, another man said, "I'll help you" and his face changed too. I screamed, "Someone help me." Then a sheriff approached me and said, "What's wrong?" I responded, "Someone is trying to get my baby." He stated, "I know you cannot hide because this is bigger than you." The next day at work my supervisor asked to speak to me in private and said the exact words. I was stunned.

A month earlier I had traveled to Washington, DC for training for my job. While traveling on the plane, I relaxed in my seat with my eyes closed; I was not asleep. I saw clearly three images: first appeared a snake, then followed by the deceased Pope John Paul II, and last was my husband's face looking charred and disfigured. I immediately began to pray and when my flight landed, I phoned my home to speak with him to see if everyone was okay. The vision was confusing and frightening. I did not understand most of these visions until many years later, I heard the voice in a dream say, "She is the little girl that will lead her deceased ancestors."

After I returned safely from my trip, I mentioned to my husband what I experienced during my flight to Washington. My dreams and visions continued like clockwork, always at the time before sunrise. Then my father died eleven months later, and I was completely lost. We always spent quality time together and even though I relocated I constantly communicated with him through phone calls and weekend excursions to return to the place where most of my fondest memories were, apart from my birthplace. I am a true country girl at heart, being the oldest child of my father and mother, I would listen to my elders attentively. I witnessed a lot of kind acts my dad did for family and strangers. I guess I followed in his footsteps. Most of all of my great-aunts and uncles, would whisper to me, "My dear, you have a special gift. Later in life you will know how to use it." I did not understand back then, hearing those words from many relatives, until after my father died and I visited one of his mother's sisters. During our visit, she began to talk about what a good man my father was, especially how he helped others throughout their lives. She went on to say, "My child, hand me your hand." I did without hesitation, and she touched it and said, "You have a gift." Within minutes, she changed the conversation to ask me what I have been doing lately. This visit was a few years after my father's untimely death from pancreatic cancer. Because I was not aware of his illness, it took me a long time to cope. Three days before his death he called me on a telephone from his hospital room and asked me to come right away. I immediately made arrangements to leave and arrive at the hospital where he was admitted in Beaumont, Texas.

My father worked for the City of Beaumont in the Water and Sewer Department for twenty-eight years and was a supervisor upon his death in 1998. My father was the backbone to his immediate family and extended family members. My dad was a multitasker and sportsman. He relocated to Cleveland, Ohio, where most of his family members from his mother's side would work on government roads and drive trucks in the early sixties. I recall when I was a little girl that my father had received a major surgery that was "very critical" and he almost lost his life when he was working away. Today I still do not know what happened forty years ago. Perhaps it was his test and he was spared by the Almighty to continue to raise his family and make an impact on people's lives. He was a simple man with few needs, a devoted husband, and a supportive father. The Creator in his infinite wisdom knew that my father had done all that was required of him on earth and it was time for him to take a sabbatical. Everyone from our large family clan came to see him during his last hours of life. He was loved by many, and I held my father's hand before his spirit left his body. It was a traumatic experience for me, never knowing what he wanted to tell me that day. He was receiving cancer treatment and slipped into a coma, but I was in denial because I felt that he would awaken, similar to my own experience five years earlier when I was in a coma and given another chance at life. I consider my father a complete servant of the Creator. While living with his grandfather, Sylvester Colligan, he enjoyed life on the range with cattle and plentiful persimmon tree, the etymology of which means "God's pear" or "divine fruit," I also note that this fruit is called the "Sharon fruit" (named after the Sharon plain in Israel). I heard a story from his cousin, Eva, mentioning that my dad was as a "starry-eyed skinny little boy who was occasional sick due to breathing problems." He would get tired during their bicycle rides to the town to get goods. While she would sit on the handle bars he would peddle them to the country store a few miles away with a pillow sack to carry the purchased items. She was bigger than him and a tomboy with strength, growing up on a farm. My dad would say in a low chuckling laugh, "I cannot pedal the both of us back home, Eva. I'm out of breath." She stated, "Then you should have stayed back." He said, "I know, but I wanted to come." This is only an example of the display of love we have for each other and the lengths the clan will go to support each other during their adolescent years. I contacted cousin Eva often to hear stories about our families. She mentioned to me one day that many males in their family had Cherokee nicknames. These names are associated with ancient corn festivals in Cherokee culture. I would hear stories from my grandmother that the witches and bogeyman would haunt all of the male Colligan offspring. I remember spending summers at my dad's mothers house. She would tell us how the witches would ride on my grandfather's back at night while he slept. The identical thing happened to my father too, and then my brother when he was about ten years old. The priest came to form an exorcism in our family home. I must say a lot of unexplained phenomenon have surrounded our family for many generations. I've had encounters of spirits during my sleepwalking when I was a child. But for some strange reason, the sleepwalking stopped for a period of years and started back again. In the fall of 1998, after my father's burial I dreamt of people during prehistoric times running along with wooly mammoths and the earth shaking in a cave and seeing myself in the center as an onlooker. I could not grasp the meaning of the recent visions. Within three days after my dad died, I saw an elderly man wearing a long white robe with a white beard standing to the right on my family's land. The man put his hand in a fountain of water, and the snake came out and bit his hand. The man looked at me smiling and a few seconds his face browsed my father. The snake began to come after me and followed me while I began to run with my younger sister to the edge of the yard. I shouted to her, "Let's climb the fence to get away from the snake." She helped me up over the fence and I reached out to her with my hand, but she stayed back. The snake crossed over and I entered a stream of water and luminous light and lost my left shoe and lied under the water able to see the snake transform into two men dressed in black. One man picked up my left shoe and began looking around but could not see me underneath the water.

One day on my way to work, I looked up in the sky and I saw a small white dove high in the heavens. I was in total awe!

In November 1999, I dreamt that I was at my mother's home and I went to get something out of my car parked on the side of the house. When I went outside, I saw a swarm of black birds flying above, and one of them began to fly near me, so I got in the car and closed the door. The bird tried to hit the glass on my window but did not come in. My mother was looking out of the window and called my husband, and he came outside and the bird started to fly near him. Tuesday morning, December 21, 1999, I had a dream I was somewhere with my family and we were outside looking at the dark sky and black birds were flying around everywhere. I made a comment, "The birds are cold and are going south for the winter." Then suddenly I was lying down, gravitating in mid-air, then a man appeared and I was lowered. He began walking next to my side, dressed all in black, and I said, "Hello, Father (priest)," he immediately placed his hand on my head and a large black bird sat on top of my head and I could not move. I began praying to God, and within minutes, the man and bird were gone. I jumped out of bed at my mother's home and looked at the time and phoned my husband. He told me to pray and try to go back to sleep until the morning light. I resumed praying until I fell back to sleep and I saw myself somewhere playing a video game and someone instructing me to shoot the target and a red light appeared. While playing, I was trying to hit a large rock and a lion began to run and hide behind it. I stopped playing and I became afraid, the lion came out and stood on the top of the rock, which was a mountain. I was standing on a white cloud and I looked down at the ground and saw an elephant standing along with people. My spirit returned to my body and I awakened.

During the beginning of December, I dreamt that I visited relatives out of town, in Louisiana and I was to return home to report to work after the weekend. I enjoyed myself with cousins, and when it was about time for me to return home for work, no one wanted to take me back. I had spent the majority of my money and began walking to an airport, where a little boy gave me a bike. On my way home I met a homeless man and a little boy standing in front of a hotel, and I began to cry. The man smiled and said, "What's wrong?" I stated, "I'm trying to get home," and he said, "Don't worry" and gave me six or seven dollars. I was excited like it was a lot of money. He said, "Hurry and catch the subway. You will make it home on time." I crossed an overpass, caught the subway, and got home in time for work and reported for duty to perform student searches at a charter school. I began searching a little girl's pocket and found a bottle of lotion, and told her, you cannot have this in your possession, it is considered contraband.

The next morning, Monday, December 6, 1999, the same little girl I saw in my dream was being searched by a coworker next to me, and I told her, check her right pocket carefully. My coworker found a bottle of lotion on the same little girl I performed the search on in my dream. I began to feel a sense of disconnection with my job because of the constant power struggles amongst coworkers. A coworker of mine confirmed my feelings by stating, "Be careful, there are many people who do not like your position as a crisis instructor," I never gave it a second thought. However, I witnessed the strangest encounter the next day at work. I saw someone I choose not to name. He had a dark cast over him and appeared to be lifeless. I felt a shiver when we passed each other walking down the corridor. I felt a strange energy, and left early, then the next morning I decided to call into work from feeling weak. I was phoned later at home and was informed that our administrator was just murdered.

After returning back to work I continued to train new hires in crisis intervention. During my presentations at work people would tell me, "You have a gift because your eyes have a light that beams and transfers a peaceful aura surrounding you." One lady told me she was a previous minister and that she had a dream about me. She said, "You will help many people in your life." I smiled and said, "I have been doing that most of my life." A few months later, I came to work and I had my injury. My mother came down to assist me and my husband with my daily chores. I was not able to move around much due to having excruciating pain in my back and hip. During my prolonged bed rest I began reading the Holy Qur'an daily. I began to feel peaceful and the pain in my back would diminish for periods while my reading continued. I prayed for a healthy baby after learning I was pregnant from an exam performed by my primary physician. My pregnancy was well as expected, with my scheduled routine checkups. Also, my younger sister had just relocated and moved in with me to help me around my home. My mother remained for a little while and returned home. One evening my sister and I were watching TV, and I mentioned to her that I was feeling tired and the baby was moving a lot, and then we both looked at the television showing a car commercial, but the caption read, "Go soak your uterus in the tub." We both could not believe what we just read. She is a veteran who worked in communications in the army for over ten years. We both agreed that it had to be someone secretly watching us and collecting information. She mentioned to me that when my husband picked her up from the bus station, two helicopters followed and hovered over them while he was driving. She said it scared her and then the helicopters retreated and went away. Weeks had gone by and my water broke while the weather was bad. Shortly after, I had my first son eleven days before the 9/11 tragedy. I recall experiencing high fevers and being released three days after from the hospital after my son was born. I decided to name him a name that signified peace because he aided me with peace after my untimely injury on the job. I prayed daily, thanking God for a son after having two beautiful daughters. I recall having problems nursing him due to my weakness and fever that exacerbated into a high degree and I fell asleep during that afternoon, I saw my mother-in-law, Haja, dressed in a deep green *Ashoke* wrap, leaning forward and pampering my son and she responded, "My daughter get up." I woke up and saw my mother standing near me and I was soaked from the fever and walked toward the bathroom. My husband was in deep prayer in another room. Shortly after, the remains of the afterbirth fell out. I suspected something was wrong when my stomach remained so large and firm, but the nurses at the hospital where I delivered my son stated to me, "You're fine. We've massaged your stomach." My intuition made me ask again because I did not feel right. My firstborn son was a gift and was born during a time of inspiration in my life, with the beginning of my earthly test. He was given a name from Nigeria, the customary practices of his father's kinship. But my mother-in-law named our daughter after her.

Alhaja was from the little town of Iseyin from the
house of a noble Muslim cleric and her family were
known as the original weavers of Hebrew cloth.

During my pregnancy, my eldest son was exposed to music and
I read many stories to him, while he was in my womb. Also, I ate
fish daily, just like my family members did. My dad would fish with
large nets and catch about every fish one could name and sometimes
a few gators. Throughout my pregnancy, rarely did I eat any meat.
I would often go with a friend to eat my usual dish of salmon and
spinach. I think it is why my son dislikes salmon today. I nurtured
him and spoiled him rotten. I did the exact same thing for all of my
children and never made differences among any of them. But when he
was born, it was a prelude to my new beginning with my search for my
destiny. My relationship with my Creator became intense, with days
of questioning like before, when I lost my father. Now I was shortly to
enter a milestone. There's a saying that goes, "A fool at forty is a fool

for life." I was thirty-eight at the time and I began withdrawing slowly from many family gatherings.

Like clockwork, my dreams and visions resumed. I saw my son around the age of four, and he called out to me and said, "Mommy, look under Granny's house. There is a large snake," and he had a javelin in his hand and threw it at the large snake and it pierced it in the midsection of its body. The snake appeared to be dead. As usual, I began my habit of helping others with traditional healing through diet change and natural remedies. I wanted to share my story of healing and sense of wellness with all who were interested.

In 2005, I had a dream that I was traveling with my family in a car and everyone fell into a body of water and I began to say, "I seek refuge with Allah from Satan and his regime." Furthermore, I said "Laih la ila la... There is no other God but Allah!" Then I heard the Azan being recited, and I repeated it and I immediately looked over to my left and saw one big crow joined by two smaller crows. Then I heard the words, "My child, what's wrong? Rise up. I have forgiven you for all the sins you committed and the ones in the past!" I then saw myself in my bedroom with my husband and my two sons. I then walked toward the window and I touched something sticky with my foot. When I began to back up, a spider crawled towards me. As I moved, it followed me, and I tried to hit it with a stick and it became hard. I noticed my baby son slide off the bed, and the spider circled around him and I ran toward him. The spider touched my other son and touched my left foot. All praises belong to the Creator! Anajatjaguar received true guidance and protection. My enemies are beneath my feet.

On March 15, 2005, I stood firm in my trials and tribulations for ten years. Today, I am rejoicing and celebrating my journey through the test. Safinat Anajat, the little boat that weathered a rocky storm to reach high plains was guided to safety, to stand tall at the highest mountaintop receiving spiritual guidance. My rites of passage was a spider touching my feet, a manifestation that I associated with the Holy Surat, Al-Ankabut, which asserts that only Allah can easily create.

My spiritual gift allowed me to pray for others during their transition from earth. I was contacted and asked to speak with my uncle over the phone for a brief few minutes, in 2015, during the month of June.

He told me some things I'd rather not disclose. However, he stated, "I remember your visits among the family years ago trying to help us to live a healthy life by changing our diets." When I had returned from Africa in 1997, many of my family alienated themselves from me. Someone very close to me accused me of witchcraft and It hurt my heart. I just wanted to share my experience and a new way of eating and taking natural herbs to live a healthier life. Within minutes of our phone conversation, I told my uncle, "Do not worry about the life you lived prior, ask God to forgive you and try to be a better person to yourself and others." He asked me what he should say. I responded, "Allah [God] is one and remember that always. He has no partners and deserves our worship." He repeated after me saying, "Allah is one." Then I heard silence and one of his sons said he had just died after speaking with me. The following year, to be exact, from 2006 to present, I have had visions often of deceased family members and other faces I've never met before. These spirits would ask me to pray for them and help them get to the light.

After each dream, I would be weak after my soul returned to my body. I could not understand what was happening to me. At first, I was afraid to mention my dreams and visions with family with the fear of being labeled as crazy. I had an active lifestyle and considered myself healthy. Although, my personal and professional life was filled with around the clock activities, I still made time to be involved in community service work. I was physically fit prior to my back injury, but after the injury I was no longer in the same shape I was before. I was unable to have conventional surgery due to a tumor that was on my lumbar, a congenital birth defect called a hemangioma, in which clusters of blood vessels interfere with blood supply. After learning about my condition, I was in denial about my current health status. Eventually, after much grieving of my health condition and the fear of the unknown, I became reclusive and refused to seek treatment. Finally, I was diagnosed with depression and was referred to a behavioral therapist to work on my issues. I believe one's enculturation is about the different influences on our environment that shape who we are and our belief system. How we react can affect our thought process and emotions which can affect our wellbeing. Truly, my experiences serve as a testimony of the trials I have faced. I have traveled this vast earth and acquired a lot of material wealth along the way. Moreover, it is all superficial to a spirit like myself, knowing the wisdom that I know now. My knowledge is in a different plane. All my basic needs, according to a hierarchy, is fulfilled. The plan is not about self but for all people.

People have mingled and lived peacefully within their nations until great powers devised plans to disrupt this peace. Like other powers the Vatican made claims through lands throughout the world under "religious pretense". Like Africa, Louisiana has massive amounts of rich fertile land. Consequently, colonial life was established to promote settlers to have opportunities of a better life in America. The *Atakapa Doomsday* book written by Glen R. Conrad includes land grants etc., in St. Martinville, Louisiana, including St. Landry Parish, where the Vatican held and controlled the riches of minerals and precious stones in Louisiana. Did the British throne hire a royal land surveyor to establish land grants and devise a plan to wipe out a nation of people that spoke a dialect similar to ancient Egyptians that traveled from other continents? African populations were growing due to the slave trade in many different countries. History repeated itself the continue enslavement of generations of Africans, our forefathers from the beginning of civilization. They crossed the Atlantic slave trade in bondage to toil for their masters and became members of a society where segregation and discriminatory practices were accepted. Little did they know the plight of injustices was interwoven in the New World. "Creole culture rebirthed its image and deep roots predating back during the black settlement named "Freetown" in the colony of Sierra Leone, founded by three groups of black settlers from England, Nova Scotia, and Jamaica." Sierra Leone became a great cultural melting pot of the world just like Louisiana. Its population of different blends of people with various cultures originating from all over the world can still be seen today. Are the stories about a tribe of ancient Indians named the Atakapa real or a myth? Nonetheless, research has proven their existence: however, most people never knew they existed. In fact, the Atakapas truly lived and were once a part of American history. Furthermore, they truly exist in our society, indeed, blended into a multiracial and multicultural background. That would not be evident to the general population due to intermingling with descendants of many other tribes and emigrants, who settled in S.W. Louisiana and S.E. Texas and historically lived along the Gulf of Mexico. Paleo Indians were some of the first inhabitants living in small nomadic groups of Louisiana wandering the land, identified as the ancestors of the Atakapa tribe. They hunted bison, deer, rabbit, and other small animals. Their homes were simple structures and their clothing was made from the skins of animals while the bones were made into tools. To be exact, the Atakapa Indians mimicked their diets identical to their ancestors, the Paleo Indians, who were trekkers in the lands of the Americas, the New World, from the Bering Strait and Eurasia, into North America thousands of years ago. Many Atakapa descendants did ancestry genealogy projects to reclaim their lost heritage taken by the sub planters who invaded their land. The Atakapa Indians have the same blood types and genetics of ancient Indians who walked the earth during the first part of the millennium, according to ancestry DNA results: "The only populations with Diego positive people may be Native American and East Asians. This nonrandom distribution pattern fits well with the hypothesis of an East Asian origin for Native Americans. To be specific, racial classification often has more to do with cultural and historical distinctions than it does to biology".

The theory that claims the Atakapa tribe was destroyed is strictly anecdotal. Likewise, the fabulous bird, the "Phoenix," which destroys itself every 500 years in a fire, only to rise again from its own ashes, is ludicrous. The myth serves as a good literary device but lacks scientific evidence in comparison to findings supporting the 500-year-old remains of a body found by the Texas Archaeology Study Association, having genetic markers like the Atakapa Indians. The stories circulating affirmed the Atakapa tribe's existence remained concealed for centuries to be indeed a true story of the forgotten Indians.

In fact, the history revealed by a former priest, tribal leader, historian, and linguist for the Atakapa tribe research involved decades of revitalizing the heritage by educating the descendants about the rich culture tucked away in the Smithsonian Institute located in Washington, DC. The study was conducted by Albert Gatschet and John Swanton around the 1900s to write an Atakapan language book. Over the next seventy years or more, the United States government claimed the Atakapa people who served the U.S.A. in all its wars were eradicated by diseases and poverty off the face of this earth. Truly the Atakapas' identity was concealed for generations to prove a theory that lacked sufficient evidence. In fact, American society must reject the null hypothesis about the Atakapas' existence, based on scientific evidence the Atakapa descendants do exist and have always existed scattered among a multicultural society. An alternative hypothesis revealed later scientific evidence of DNA mapping, and research linking the descendants of the Atakapa to their predecessors. The hunters and gatherers, who once roamed this land with gigantic beasts, evolved through adaptive behavior centuries later to coexist with Europeans who schemed to thin out their ancestral bloodline. Through consensual and nonconsensual marriages, the races mixed to acquire the Atakapas' land through pretense when performing government census to account for people through racial discrimination. Therefore, the Atakapa tribe called themselves "ee-SHAK," which translates as "The People" who had lived in secrecy involving complex issues in a multicultural society. Consequently, a "complex combination of cultural, ancestral, societal, and symbolic meaning placed burdens on most Indian families to teach their children to maintain their true identity."

Tradition and culture place an emphasis on belonging to the family clan. Knowing one's heritage is an essential factor in a Native American's life. Teaching their ways of living to their people is a moral obligation among kinsmen. For instance, to preserve their culture, the male would take his nephews (tens) from his family (shakishak) and develop their manhood by taking them fishing, catching gator, and hunting deer and rabbit. Even centuries later in modern society, the Atakapas continue the same practices as their ancestors who were forgotten in American history. When the men returned from their journey of hunting and fishing, the women prepared and cooked the food. Also living close to marshland and coastal waters, the Atakapas thrived on seafood as a main dish among other foods. The Atakapas were resourceful like their ancestors before them. Once everyone had finished eating, a family elder would tell a story or joke for entertainment. The Atakapas took pride in their native clothing, which included a variety of materials, especially breechcloth with fringes and fancy adornments not limited to beads and feathers. Annual powwows were time for family to bond during gatherings and tribal ceremonial. They believe their deceased ancestors could reach them in spirit, which happened in my case. Due to the geographical climate, the Atakapas gathered many herbs like the lotus flower which is known for its healing properties.

Belonging to the tribe is unique in its own rights as is a child who belongs to his maternal and paternal parent. Native pride exists in the heart of each member and it has been passed down through generations. In the past centuries, the shaman performed religious ceremonies and rituals in their native tongue and cured the sick, using traditional medicine versus conventional medicine. Many family members adopted the old ways of life and continued to use natural remedies.

Despite hardships, they cohesively joined with other members to fight for their constitutional rights as Americans, while some members remain out of sight, battling demons from the past struggling for inner peace.

Moreover, they were shunned from their ancestral lands through trickery and forceful encounters with individuals who had no respect for mankind due to the thirst and lust for "fertile and spacious land flowing with milk and honey". The Atakapas realized they were forgotten in a newly developed land thought to be extinct by the federal and state government.

"[Europeans] put us in poverty," said Edward Chretien Jr., principal chief of the Atakapa-Ishak Nation, which formed in 2006. "They wanted your land. If they didn't kill you for your land, they drove you into hiding... it was shameful to be Native American".

The Atakapa people met secretly at segregated meeting places, unknown to the outside world, trying to provide for their families. In addition to maintaining dignity and identity no matter the cost, the Atakapas' moral code teaches love and preservation of a deep-rooted culture that has surpassed the test of time.

We the Atakapas were reared to be self-sufficient, humane, and aware of all our surroundings, including others, creatures, nature, and the environment that our Creator has created for humanity. Throughout my entire childhood life, I learned about my rich culture while interacting only with family. The family elders would say, "We are protecting our own after many attempts of genocide." When I reached adulthood, I was told by my parents, "We never reveal our identity if we want to LIVE... Never talk about it."

Chief Michael Amos (great-uncle of Anajatjaguar), former chief of the Atakapas, said, "tensa, my dear daughter, we're in a spiritual warfare because we are the true blood lineage of the tribe of Juda! And we are the People of the Book."

The Atakapa descendants filed their petition for federal recognition to preserve their culture and history.

Although the Atakapas were decimated by infectious diseases after European contact and declined as a tribe, survivors joined other tribes and lived in secrecy and poverty over centuries. The Atakapas exists through living generations who have begun their journey to reclaim all that was stripped from their ancestors.

Chief Michael Amos was dedicated to fighting for the rights of our families to receive federal recognition from the United States government. In a short excerpt from Indian Country News, my uncle stated, "It will give us our identity back and we can do things for our people and bring back our culture and heritage." The Smithsonian Institute sent linguist Albert Gatschet to the Gulf Coast during the late 1800s to write an Atakapan language dictionary before the last known native speaker died, noted by McNeese State University history professor Ray Miles.

Furthermore, the Atakapa legacy can be seen throughout the different areas in Louisiana. The Atakapa warrior statue in front of St. Martin de Tours Catholic Church, in St. Martinville serves as testament to their rich culture. According to history, Opelousas and Atakapa Districts were home to the largest group of rural free people of color before the Civil War in Louisiana. The Atakapa and the Opelousas Districts were named after two Native American tribes that lived in south Louisiana at the time of European contact. Europeans and their slaves first settled in the Atakapa District in the 1750s along the Bayou Teche. The first records of Africans in the region are of the slaves owned by André Masse. Before his death, Masse freed his slaves, creating the nucleus of the district's free people of color community.

The stomping grounds of our ancestors from the
Sunset and Sunrise people, the Atakapa Indians.

The Bayou Teche, known to many as a pathway to life.

Edward Chretien, "Chief Crying Eagle"

Janice Ryder Shuff, former Panther Band council
member of the Atakapa-Ishak Nation.

One day while visiting the Olivier Plantation a female tour guide made a comment that I had sat on the veranda, exactly as my grandmere would do, while sipping her tea every morning. The Olivier Plantation was where my fourth great-grandmother lived, who was a slave named Benedicta. She was a beautiful woman referred to as a *griffon tres mix blood* and as the mistress of the plantation she was emancipated by her master, Pierre Olivier. Upon the death of Pierre Olivier, my great-grandmother bought her son, Norbert, from the succession sale of Pierre's estate in 1841. During my tour of the Olivier Plantation in St. Martinville in 2013, I visited the grounds where many of my ancestors worked on the sugar plantation for the Olivier's, who ironically had family members married into my father's family clan. The South was painted with subtle racial profiling depending upon the color of ones' skin.

My sister accompanied me at tribal court in Charenton, Louisiana, to inquire about our ancestors living in St. Mary Parish on the Chitimacha Reservation.

I believe in equality for all! Since when do we need tribal courts that sabotage the rights of all native people, who cannot distinguish blood,

which is one color? But the Ishak people are of all skin colors and facial features due to the intermingling of different tribes and races.

Sunset, Louisiana, is home to many Atakapa descendants who have remained within the hometown of their ancestors to continue life and trade by barter and coexist with unity and pride in their native heritage. Many of my extended family members have small gardens of vegetables and fruit trees like the generations before us maintained throughout the decades. My native hometown is Lafayette, Louisiana. My ethnic makeup consists of Atakapa, Choctaw, Chitimacha, Houma, and Cherokee, with a collaboration of other ethnicities like, German, Irish, Spanish, French, Italian, African, and much more.

Home is where the heart is. I hail from five generations of farmers, from both my father and mother's side. I love the land where I was born.

Pictured is my Uncle Charles Colligan (farmer)

My daughter pictured next to a kumquat tree, in the path where my uncle cultivates family land where the crops are plentiful and ripe for the picking, e.g. sugarcane, fig, oranges, lemon trees, African field peas, and various fruit trees.

My great-uncle Peter Francis, whose father was from the Francis family clan, lived in the Bayou Terrebonne Parish along with my father's family, the Millers. While the Francis men were drafted during

WWI they were given the opportunity to be classified as white or to keep their Native racial identity. Many of the male descendants from my mother's side served in the armed forces and were members of the Houma Tribe.

My mother's great-grandfather, Edouard Judice Francis, was born in 1832, it was said that he was born when a meteor shower blanketed the night sky of America, called the "Night the Stars Fell." He fought on the Confederate side in company F 1st Special Battalion, Louisiana Infantry (Rightor's) and died without a plaque. Edouard Francois's wife, Francois Broussard, was the daughter of an Acadian soldier named Francois Broussard. All the Francis males were classified in the census records of 1930 as having 97.4 blood quantum in the Police Ward 4, Terrebonne, Louisiana. Moreover, my family has always been referred to as free people of color, mulatto, and sometimes referred to as a triracial person. Two of my ancestors Benedicta and Marie Pierre aka "Savage" were classified as pure-blooded Indian.

Ancestry genealogy reveals land deeds and census records listing Marie Anne Pierre "Free Quadroom," Chitimacha mayor during the time of the Louisiana Purchase in 1803, whose husband was Alexandre Billot, chief of the Chitimacha tribe in Charenton. Many of the Pierre clan still reside today in Charenton and Lewisburg. When I visited the tribal courts in 2013, an elderly woman told me that she had no knowledge of any of my family members registered with the Chitimacha tribe in Charenton or any distant relatives from the Terrebonne county known as the Houma Indians, who were trappers and fishermen that lived along the bay after being dislocated from their farmland. Nevertheless, history and my research reveals contradictory evidence. In 1880, congress began selling public land on "Bayou Little Cailou," where it was first documented. First Indian families were the Billots (of Chitimacha ancestry) and the Courteau (of Biloxi and Colapissa tribe), who were the ancestors of the Biloxi-Chitimacha-Choctaws of Louisiana, my ancestors. "From 1810 to 1920 Louisiana legally classified Indians as "people of color," this case from a ruling by the Louisiana Supreme Court in 1810, which defined "people of color" to include persons who may be descended from Indians on both sides, from a white parent or mulatto parent in possession of their freedom", like the "Old Houma" woman, my ancestor Rosalie Courteau who was a revolutionary helping her people survive.

During an Interview with a caretaker for Chretien Point, who was born in 1944 on the property, which was near Bellevue Cemetery, earlier known as an auction block for the selling of slaves. Chretien Point was the former estate of my ancestors in the 1800s, before government occupancy and later selling of the property. The mansion is now a bed and breakfast with paranormal activity witnessed by many tourists today. My actual account of seeing dead ancestors and sighting when I was a child is real! The restless spirits refuse to transition and leave the earthly plain.

This is his story of growing up on Chretien Point. He stated, "During the Civil War, our black people were slaves brought to Louisiana to work on numerous plantations throughout Louisiana. A white person would take a black woman to clean their homes and then they would abuse them. The blacks could not retaliate out of fear. Chretien Point in sunset during the war was the army base and the white men ran the Natives away. When they could not recruit most of the Natives, they decided to purchase African slaves and make an army. Later some natives were drafted. The white men told the people that they can fight in the war to see the government to own their land on paper because, they could not read or write. The white man grabbed a bunch of sticks and stuck them in the ground to claim land."

Thereupon he stated, "the white began killing Natives, and the Natives started migrating everywhere to hide." He further elaborated that "blacks could not receive an education and his mother would cry because her son could not read and write." His mother would light a candle to read, and the white overseer on the plantation would use whips or canes they used on mules to beat them as they dropped to their knees. He recalls that the overseer would threaten to kill his mother and siblings, if she taught them to read. So, they stayed on the plantation, but it was rumored that one of my ancestors named Francois Chretien, a free colored Indian child from a former slave master of Chretien Point, received a land allotment for his service in the war, and returned to try to free the people from slavery."

He also stated "many innocent lives were lost on the land. So Chretien Point is haunted, and the spirits are restless and the apparitions of the people that died on the second floor are still seen till this day. It is also mentioned that the Natives cursed the white man and said they will never prosper even though history states the mistress cursed the mansion as well. Still today, many people are afraid to travel on the old bridge or road adjacent to Chretien Point, especially during All Saints Day or All Hallow's Eve. He made a reference that the dead will walk again and states that "people say little strange doll-like figures come out at night from the woods to terrorize people."

He then stated that "After the war was over, "we found freedom at last. We had become wild people because we were so happy to be free. Now we can't stop because we have come so long, but as long as I live, I will never want to live that life again." "We got lost in the sand tracts because we never clean our feet." If God wanted "yes, sir" and "no, sir," he would have put it in our mouths. "The white man is putting us down instead of living a life like that he'd rather not live. It was a hard life during slavery time, and the white man takes everything and don't give but a nickel or a dime and you cannot even feed your family. The little children are lost and they don't want the black children to have an education to make it in this life."

"They grab everything in life, good and bad, trying to survive with the little that their family can provide for because everything cost— even the land that was once free and belonged to all Native people. A black man's next of kin chose to live as white to survive. A black man has nowhere to turn for help but to be lost in his mind because the end result is not in man's control; it's in God's control."

"The black man cuts grass to take care of his family, but grass does not grow every day. I know from experience as a groundskeeper and driver for the previous owner of the Chretien Point, when Marilyn Monroe came to town to make a movie and her boyfriend (not named) took her for a ride. He further mentioned that "he remembers seeing Marilyn during her stay at Chretien Point." Rumor has it that her uncle was looking for the big picture on the wall of the mansion. The boss man wanted to change the air vent, and he needed his assistance to change it and to their surprise a hidden portrait of Marilyn Monroe fell and shattered on the floor. The boss man stated, "When you get finished, throw it away." He stated that "he kept the picture for thirty-seven years." The picture resides in an undisclosed location to many. He discreetly told me the location and that he knew that a little girl from the blood lineage of Natives of the land would tell the story about her ancestors.

A patent for land owned by my ancestor, Francois D. Chretien.

It is true that the Chretien family owned slaves, but thanks to our Creator, we know the ways of life are much different now compared to how it was during slavery. I try to educate my children that our past history has many scars, but we are on a journey of healing to understand why the world is like it is, and people are pawns to disparities on the earth. It is a common fact, "Law of nature: the stronger overpower the weak!" In 1851 Josette Chretien, a free woman of color owned a slave named Auguste and purchased him for $1,275.

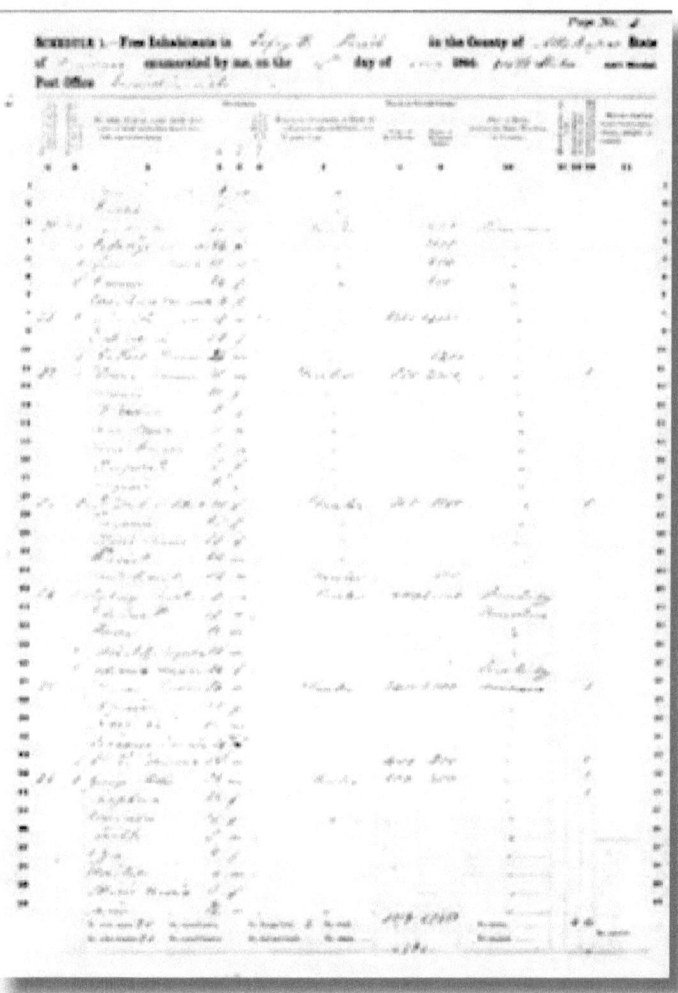

My mother's uncle, Pierre Francis, was age five. During the time of this turbulent year, most of my family members endured hardships and trials, in contrast to the pleasant life their ancestors tasted for a short time. The Francis family hailed from Spain. When Louisiana became a state in 1812, ancestors of the people we know to be the "Houma redbones" came to the area when it was still a territory. They first came to the South in the Lafayette area and moved to the west and central part. A redbone is a person of mixed racial heritage, who is a member of a group that defines its relationship to the dominant culture in a certain way, with a racial mix of two or more of the following: Native American, European, Caucasian, Asians, English, French, Irish, Welsh or Portuguese, Spanish, Moor, Turk and many of the various Negroid subgroups. Francois D. Chretien was my fourth great-grandfather on my father's side of the family. He was born in 1783 in Opelousas, Louisiana. He was married to Pelagii Carriere Chretien. They had a daughter named Josette. The Chretien clan owned several plantations during the 1800s when the cotton crop reigned as lifeline to the state's economy. Rumor has it that when Josette was mistress of the plantation, an unidentified carpetbagger decapitated her head and she roams the grounds, along with other spirits of former slaves. That were killed during the antebellum period. In fact, my bloodline thrived on the lands of the Atakapa. Both generational lineages were born and raised on Chretien Point. Moreover, my mother and many of her family members, who were farmers and sharecroppers. So history has it that my father's family were wealthy landowners, allowing the free inhabitants who were already occupants of the land to have lease agreements to cultivate the land. Power and privilege forced many uneducated family members to sign away their land rights to the Europeans without comprehending the legal transaction. Also, during the Civil War the inheritance of my matrilineal female members had been controlled by their husbands. Native families frequently encouraged their daughters to marry European traders.

My third great-grandfather Don Louis Charlot on my father's side migrated from France in the 1800s, and married an Indian woman named Alexandrine Chretien. Her mother was Pelagii Carrier, married to Francois Chretien. Pelagii was the daughter of Louis Carriere (1738–1814), and her mother's name was Louise Gradenigo (1778–1865). The female patrilineage traces back to a noble Venetian explorer from Venice, Italy, who set sights on making a life across the seas from the quaint little isles to the deep rivers of the Mississippi Delta to acquire new fortune and fame in a desolate land in Post Opelousas, Atakapa District, where there were indigenous people living in a multicultural society. Also, Francois Chretien, Patriarch Joseph Chretien (1775–

1812), hails from Trois-Riveres, Quebec, Canada, and resided in Opelousas until his death at the old age of eighty-seven. The Chretien clan lived on the shores of North America since the early 1600s.

The copy of the land deed was passed down from my third great-grandmother, Josette Chretien, from her father, Francois D. Chretien in 1850. Josette was twenty-eight when she departed from Havre, Spain, on the ship named James N. Cooper and arrived on December 24, 1846, in New Orleans. She lived with her parents until she became the mistress of Chretien Point in St. Martin, Louisiana, where she controlled the second sugarcane plantation.

During the Napoleonic period, land was noted as arpents and passed to heirs. I met a law clerk in the Opelousas Courthouse that observed me researching old dusty torn land deeds in plat survey books in the basement. The young gentlemen asked if I was a descendant to the Chretien's. I responded yes! He stated that he heard, "Josette was beheaded during the Civil War on the property, and some people think her ghost haunts the land." See illustration below of a chart explaining units of length and area used in France, Louisiana, and Canada.

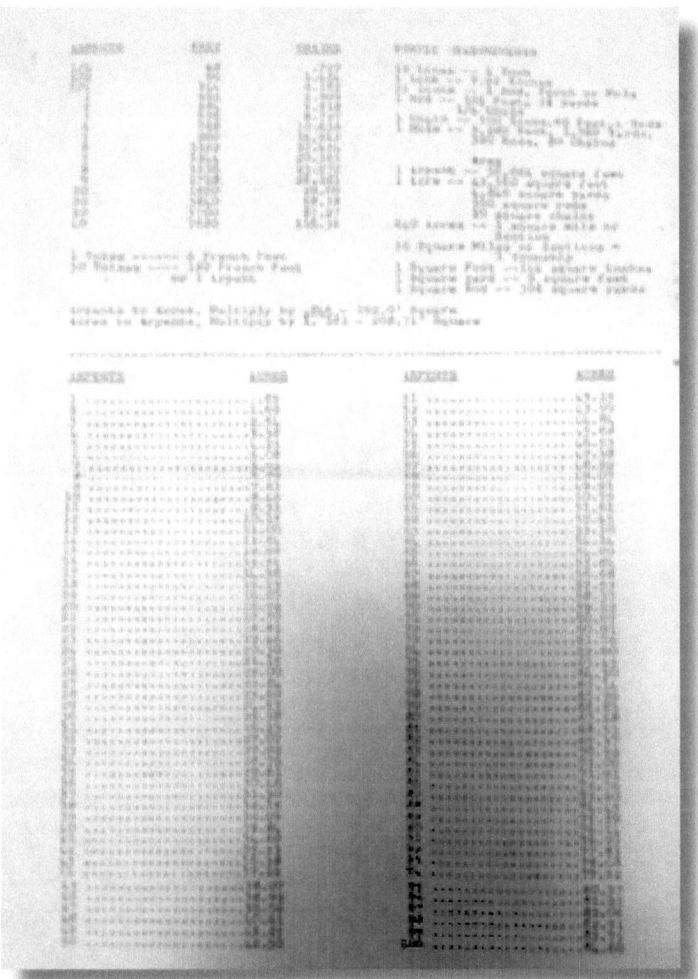

Many of my ancestors received land allotments, generally 160 acres for each head of the family and 80 acres for each single person over 18 years of age. My ancestor, Alexandrine Chretien, received certain tracts or parcel of land with all the buildings and improvements thereon situated at Coulee Croche in the parish measuring 95.8 acres. My great-grandmother, Eva Charlot, the eleventh daughter and wife of Sylvester Colligan, had lot#11 of a plot as her share, measuring 8.5 acres.

My great-grandmother on my father's side, Alexandrine Chretien Charlot, had also been referred to as Alexandrine Lematte. I heard she was the daughter of a soldier who forced himself on her mother during the wartime, a too-familiar story among Native women and soldiers. On the other hand, perhaps the stories were created to account for the Spanish blood found in our DNA.

Nonetheless, it is what it is in the South. Skeletons and deep past secrets taken to the grave to avoid ridicule and gossip among generations. But history repeats itself, and those buried facts have to resurface to answer the questions needed to put the spirits to rest. My mission to learn about my heritage was driven by my vision on June 6, 2012. An elderly woman appeared, dressed in a long white gown, with two long, red braided plaits, with a little girl facing the opposite side out of view. The lady was sitting in a chair and seemed to be waiting on someone. The right side of where she was seated was a large tree. She told me to eat the leaf and it will give me a long life. Then she began to walk away while the moonlight shining down bright.

I began to notice a form of ID or something on the chair where she sat. I picked up the piece of paper and followed her and said, "You forgot something." She said, "No, it belongs to you!" I looked at it, and it was my picture ID with my name on it. I looked puzzled and she said, "You are of Indian descent. Now go and claim your inheritance."

When I was doing some of my research in 2013, my ancestor, Alexandrine Chretien, wife of Don Louis Charlot, would appear to me along with other deceased family members. The folklore is that all the family members in Louisiana are all blood relations and some are cursed because of the cruelty invoked and the killings of innocent people.

Chretien Point is surrounded by a white picket fence that shrouds the perimeter of the boundaries from outsiders entering the grounds, where some of my extended family members resided and sharecropped for hundreds of years. Reflecting on my shared summer vacations visiting both grandparents, I remember one of my maternal uncles picking us up in a truck across the tracks where my father's family had remained on many acres and maintained their scheduled farm shares. Despite the weeks of being divided between both family houses, I enjoyed my time spent with family. I was around seven or eight years of age when I picked cotton as a child, sometimes with splinters in my fingers from the prickly thorns of blessed thistle, a medicinal remedy, after being planted and harvested it produces cotton for the comfort of society. Wow! Rhetorically speaking, I cannot believe during the time I was picking cotton on the land decades earlier before the Civil War that my father's ancestors reaped abundance of economic wealth and status until the new masters occupied and took the spoils of war.

After dusk had fallen, I would jump out of the truck that my uncle was driving. A force would draw me to the gate to gaze at the tattered ruins of Chretien Point. Around the back part of the mansion, my mother's father did tenant farming. I would climb up on the fence and speak with deceased ancestors wandering around, who were looking for a way to the light. My uncle would shout and say "Stop, come back before the ghost gets you." I was not afraid of anything because I encountered a lot in the spiritual realm as a child, never knowing this place has blood ties to my flesh. Now as an adult, I understand a lot of manifested pain that some of my ancestors endured. My journey has taken me to spiritual awareness by the Creator, and affirming the light has made things clearer and the spiritual cleansing has taken effect. Challenges in my lifetime have defined my purpose of existence to give back to humanity. I've fully bloomed like the lotus flower signifying enlightenment! While my past life before enlightenment, was closed like the bud of the lotus. Continuing in my midlife crisis, I emerged partly open but seeking opportunities still hidden beyond ordinary sight. My spirit quest began from the moment I saw my deceased ancestors in dreams and visions repeatedly over my lifetime. I would even sleepwalk as a child and finding myself asleep outside on the ground. Furthermore, this act continued throughout my adulthood. I would wake up to be outside of my home without remembering walking outside for any apparent reason. I know from the time when I was about seven years old, I would climb trees and sit and begin to stare into space. I was a curious child by nature, always asking a lot of questions and being around my elders. One day after a family gathering, my dad took the wishbone from a chicken and told me to break it, and I had the larger part. So he said, "Go stand outside and look upon the stars and make your wish." I was so excited and asked God to let me be a princess and help people.

Growing up in the South, I lived a sheltered life and only interacted with members of my family. I did not enjoy going to parochial school during my youth because I experienced prejudice and discrimination through being bullied. I was called a "heathen" and had my mouth washed out with soap and stripped down to my slip for no reason. I was afraid of most of the nuns and the priest who were in charge of the school where I and my siblings attended. One day I recall being locked in a room during the time for the children to go to the grave site to pray for the dead. All I could do was pray that someone would hear me yelling and would come to my rescue. I was scared as a child to tell my parents about my physical abuse at the school. It was a horrible experience. Also, the weekly confessions speaking to a priest about things children do. I recall telling the priest, "Father, I've been a good girl and did all of my homework and helped around my home." He would say, "Confess your sins, my child, you are a sinner." I did not understand back then why I had to talk in a box to a man. But

I did as I was told. I remember the parish priest visiting our home to eat my father's cooking. He would cook a lot of Creole dishes like turtle, rabbit, deer, alligator, and fish. He would wake up in the morning around four a.m. to go hunting and fishing every weekend, the customary practices of the Cherokee male in the past. They would later jubilee during a corn festival and wear mask to frighten children into being good. Cherokee clansmen would go hunting for food and later jubilee during a corn festival.

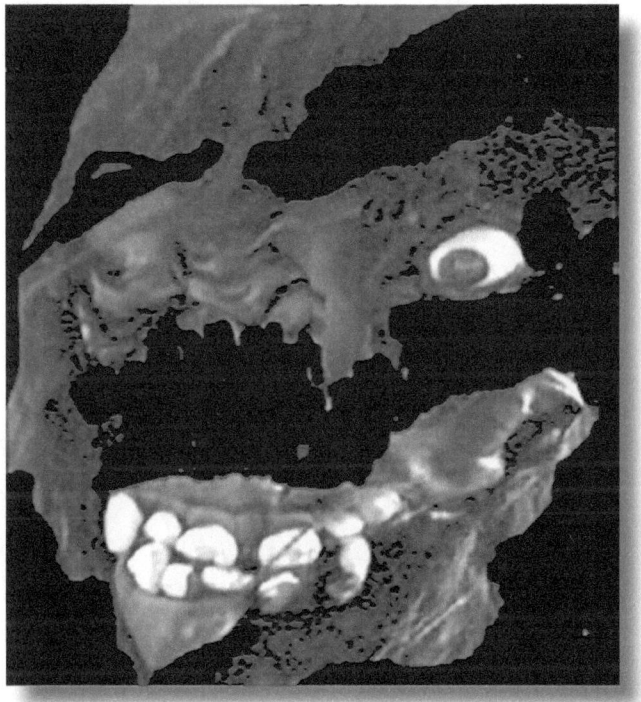

Similarly, this tradition continued with my grandmother, Emma Miller, and she passed it along to her son, Lu Lu, my dad. When the family was gathered around the table, my grandmother and dad would leave for a moment and return wearing the bogeyman mask.

My siblings and other family members would begin screaming. My grandmother would walk closer and begin to say, "Eat all of your food so the bogeyman won't get you." Similarly, in Persian culture, children who misbehave may be told by their parents to be afraid of Lu Lu, the bogeyman who eats everything up. The threat is generally used to make small children eat their meals.

What is even more scarier is that my dad scared all of our family members too with the mask. The mask was worn by my grandmother and my father, and is approximately forty years old.

My grandfather's, and heirloom kept by my father until his death. Then passed down to my uncle for safekeeping preserving the Colligan's legacy.

After all, the spirit lives on and remains around loved ones. I witness my granddad's accordion sound a tune in the exact room where most of our family enjoyment would take place. It is true, and this happened when I went to my visit the house where my grandfather lived forty years ago. My aunt brought out the accordion for me to snap a photo, and when she began to remove it from its storage, to our surprise, one of the straps was released, I heard a tune and I felt butterflies dancing in my heart. I knew it was a sign that he was there in spirit.

Part of our continuous family gatherings is for family to come from far-off places to hear the sounds of music that touch the soul. We are a proud people who are content with living by divine order, with the exception of chaos caused by social injustices across the land.

The lost tribe of Israel wandered many centuries to reach the Promised Land. We are some of the descendants of those wandering kinsmen who have mixed with tribes to produce offspring carrying different blood of one tribe of a parent that is dominant, while the other child carries the blood of the other parental family. We have been followed for decades through intimidation, to tear apart the very woven existence of a people wrapped in a mystery of tribal groups. My male lineage from my father side has confirmed my genetic breakdown of my ancestor, Jacque Charlot, of the "Mande" ethnicity, who lived from 1766 to 1848. It is presumed that he was captured during the Trans-Atlantic Slave Trade. That is how many subgroups migrated from Africa to many countries.

I remember doing my blood work in 2001, while I was pregnant and the doctor asked me if I was an Amerasian child, because of my blood type and facial characteristics. His comment would explain why my transition to public schools as a teenager I was called an "alien" and beaten by a gang of girls on the grounds of the Catholic school I attended when I was young. I recall one of my sisters running to the cafeteria to get help. The lady who was there just closed the door in her face and would not get anyone from the church to assist. My sister had to run about three miles home to get help. Fortunately, my dad was working in the neighborhood. So she met him at his truck, and he immediately came. He contacted the police department and a report was filed. But nothing ever transpired. Why did a gang of girls that I did not know come on private property and assault me for no apparent reason? Truly, the Creator knows! After, this incident, my dad purchased a Doberman pinscher who we named Joe. He would watch us and walk along with us to school. He would follow the car when we were dropped off to school. One day before class was dismissed, Joe was sitting at the edge of the ditch by the church grounds waiting for me and my siblings to get out of school. He was a real loyal dog to the family. Looking back, I've experienced a lot of cruelty as a child from strangers most of my entire life. One ordeal to the next, whether by malicious intent or unknowingly by most of my enemies. I come from a large family where considerable amount of threats have been made on their lives. However, the Colligan dynasty produced my male bloodline into a prosperous generation who could run the town wherever they lived. I met a sheriff deputy while doing my research in the courthouse in Opelousas, Louisiana. He told me that years ago, if one takes Highway 1872 leaving Opelousas and drive a few miles, down to the right is the town Frilot, Kokomo, and Latel, where my great-grandad Red Bud had many acres of land in Fateique Prairier. When I visited these areas in 2013, most of the locations are currently housed by parish churches and government landmarks. In Louisiana, you can find a church on every corner like elsewhere in many cities, with the exception of the churches being placed in different parishes, a result of the infamous Vatican rule called Code Noir. In my personal opinion, I feel strongly this was a plot of an integrated hierarchy to destroy and weaken the masses of the underdogs of civilization. My reasoning is sound, according to the 1200 documents I turned into the Indian Trust Settlement. I was compelled to do this from a vision of one of my deceased ancestors telling me to claim my Indian heritage. The master judge in charge of the proceeding informed me that I've proved extensive genealogy of my ancestors connecting to my bloodline. My DNA and blood type is another key indicator of my heritage.

The B positive blood type is derived from people who lived in the Himalaya Mountains. It first appeared in the India region of Asia, among a mix of Caucasians and Mongolian tribes known as the steppe dwellers. My granddaughter also inherited the exact blood type of our ancestors. She is pictured below in my garden, picking fresh rosemary.

In September 2011, I had a dream I was holding the moon in my lap. Then a voice said, "She is the one here for all that hear her words." My dream involved three men gathered under a tree in Africa. They were talking to each other saying, "Let's take his children from him." First, they went after his daughter and later they called his sons. The youngest said the three men were trying to do tricks around them. I cried out and my younger son responded, "Mommy, don't worry. They did not hurt me." I told their father I heard people talking about ruining his business and his relationship so they can continue to quarrel. So my husband said, "Hurry, do not be late for the program." But it was raining heavily and I was dressed in a royal purple long gown and head wrap. I said I would be soaked and decided to go back into the house. I saw a large white cat, and I sent my children back away from its presence. My husband responded, "Oh, so you have been hiding in here always." He opened the door and the cat looked back at him and walked out. He shut the door closed. People began coming, gathering around, trying to come in so they could see what was going on. "And it was said that the line of King Solomon is always guarded on the top of the mountain on the right side with lots of angels. No one or nothing can cross to the right, that is bad, but stay to the left." So I told my sister when she was trying to see what was being explained. I said, "You are a witness. Stop staying back and climb up so you can see." Immediately the people looked toward my husband and something ran toward him, it was a large buffalo and it fell over the door path, and then the cat also fell next to him in the same position. I said he was telling the truth about the buffalo. It is dead, and reporters began coming with microphones and tape recorders and discussing about writing a book about what happened.

On September 25, 2011, I dreamt that I was walking with my younger sister and my son. We were buying groceries and trying to play a lottery ticket in a store. We each gave a number and said to each other that if we would win, we would not start any disagreement between us about sharing the winnings. So my son said, "Mommy, you all sign the paper and write down your numbers." My son said he will keep the information. We saw people running and walking fast in the parking lot. The hour was getting late and a woman announced the winners of the lottery and we said, "We won." My son said, "Mommy, here is the paper," and I took it. It said "assist" and I asked my son, "Who wrote the words?" He replied, "It's from my spelling words. Allah wants us to assist people." So a lady at the customer service desk responded, "You have all the time you want to collect your money because it belongs to no one else except the both of you."

After having this vision, I reflected back on my humanitarian service over numerous years in my personal life for no monetary gain. I met a young lady back in 2007, who was from Queens, New York. One of her children was attending the same school as my eldest son. She spoke to me briefly how she'd relocated with her children for a short stay with her husband's family. I opened up my home to them. I was dealing with my own trauma, not to mention, my heart went out to her being a stranger in a new place. She confided in me about her current situation. I did my best to assist them in their time of need. Thereafter, within a few months, she returned back to her hometown. After a while, I received a letter expressing her thoughts and prayers are always sounding out my good deeds to her family.

My prayers, hard work, and dedication to family has emerged. My sons have carried down a legacy from both families of inventors. They enjoy designing games and playing with their friends. We have always encouraged and supported our children in meeting their educational goals. Much to our surprise, the boys decided to take their ideas to a higher level. They invented an educational app.

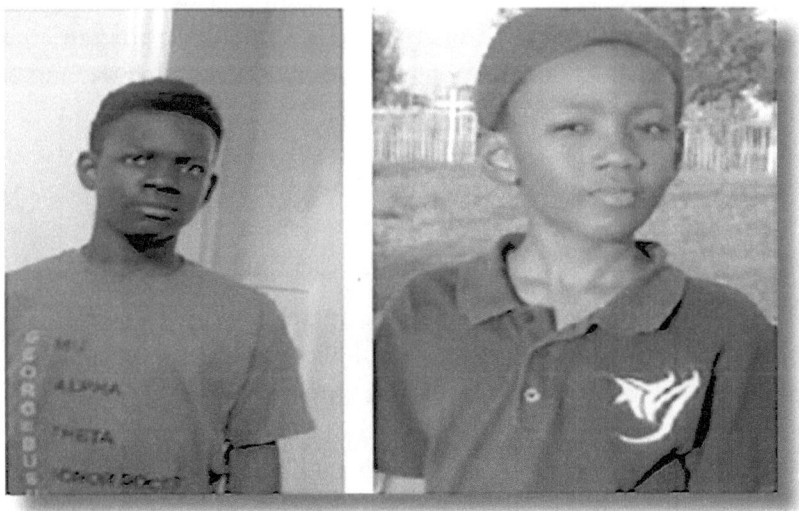

After some time, I decided to contact my uncle because of the visions I had been having since my father died. I would journal and write them down each morning. I had not seen any of my extended family after my back injury, taking care of my children, and having countless doctor appointments, until one day it hit me like a pound of bricks. I must return to the land where I was born. My reclusiveness only allowed me to interact with my immediate family on occasion out of fear of the unknown. My consistent praying let me travel to visit my uncle. When I arrived, my uncle said, "We are Native Americans and my great-uncle has filed for a petition for us to get our tribal lands back in our possession." I was really surprised because I knew deep down in my heart, the way my mother dressed me and my siblings in cultural wear, with the exception of uniforms when attending school, signified our culture. Also, my great-uncle was growing old and had done great things for the tribe. We spoke briefly on many occasions. My travel to Louisiana was a set course already planned by my Creator. My purpose was to regain my lost heritage. My family members were evasive when I mentioned that I came to inform everyone about the information of our ancestry. Most of the members from my mother's side laughed at me. It hurt my heart, but my mission would not stop. I found favor with my younger sister and uncle. I began visiting the lands and courthouses, and spoke with people who supported my endeavors. I recall speaking to an attorney in the courthouse who noticed me with massive documents reviewing at a computer desk. He ask me if I was an attorney representing any families for the Cobell Settlement. I was controlled by a force that was compelling me to try and find answers that day when I received a telephone call from my father back in 1998, telling me to come quickly because he needed to share something with me about my birth. I asked him, "Was everything all right?" He responded, "I'm in the hospital hurry so I can talk with you." Unfortunately, an hour and a half later, he fell in a coma.

I was distraught and looking for the doctor, and then a man appeared with a white coat and name tag. He looked at me and said, "Are you Stephanie?" I said, "Yes! And who are you, may I ask?" He stated, "I'm your father's doctor." I was shocked. I did not know my father was ill. We had just spent time together with the family. He was barbecuing, which was his hobby, while I watched and began telling him about my problems. As a matter of fact, he stared off for a brief moment and said to me, "Don't worry about a thing because you will be well taken care of." I said, "What do you mean, Dad?" He said, "Don't worry. Enjoy yourself." And I kissed him on the cheek and smiled, and a family member joined us and we engaged in a different topic.

Later in life, I was met with a lot of gossip by family members, telling me that I was not my father's child. I could not believe what I was hearing. Is this a joke or what is going on? I know I had not seen much of the extended family due to my living away from home, but I'm sentimental and these rumors were affecting me. I started to lose focus of why I was there and what my great-uncle, the chief, had said to me. I cried to the point of my heart hurting, having so many mixed emotions. I had a loss in time and began to remember the bad things that had happened to me throughout my lifetime. I'm not professing to be perfect in any way. But I did not ask for these atrocities to happen to me. Where do I begin?

First and most important, I have a relationship with my Creator. I know prayer has guided me through all the darkness I've been in until the light came, and guided me not to be silent any longer and play the victim role. I'll be the overcomer and face my demons from the past and present, and people who are evil and know things of my birthright and want it hidden. I will not give them the upper hand. I'll be victorious in this spiritual battle, whatever the outcome may be. I want justice for myself as well as the freedom of liberties that we as individuals are entitled to by our constitutional rights.

As human beings of this New World, I'll not let Satan take my dignity after my journey has been so hard and filled with so many trials and consequences that I've endured.

In spirit, I felt like the swan in the Aesop's fable, who was threatened with death, and burst forth into song and thus made herself known by her voice. My courage grew and I decided to join social media in 2013, after my hard work of researching my ancestors. I joined Ancestry.com and Facebook to use as a tool to connect to unknown extended family members. Once I started my genealogy research, my dreams became more detailed with known places and names. One morning before my trip, I saw a man beating the drum and chanting along the shore of the Lake Charles River. Seconds later, I saw four images, a snake, panther, heron, bear, and then three men. The last one was seated in a chair in front of two large wooden doors. I walked past them and opened the door. The next morning, I continued with my preparation to travel the next day. When I arrived in Opelousas, Louisiana, my sister took me to the tourist center to inquire about the Atakapa tribe. There a gentleman overheard me and told me that I just missed the chief of the tribe yesterday educating tourists about the tribe and their culture. He phoned a former chief of the Opelousas, Prairie tribe. He greeted me and my sister and welcomed us to his home for dinner and to discuss my mission. I showed him documents and my research on the family's lineage. He looked at my paperwork and we learned that we were related through Caroline Barker, the matriarch of the Miller clan. I decided to share with him that he was one of the chiefs in my vision, and two other men along with him. He showed me a picture of a relative who was the current chief of the tribe. I recognized him from seeing him in my vision. I said, "He is the man along with you and my great-uncle." We contacted him and he asked me to join him at a festival in St. Martinville in a couple of weeks. So I decided to continue my research and lodge at my uncle's home until that date. I attended the festival with other family members and we visited the St. Martinville Cultural Heritage Center. I returned home and began the process to submit the family paperwork for the Indian trust historical records. I was able to send in the required documents by the specified date.

The night I returned home, I dreamt that my family members gathered around looking at a document. Immediately I saw myself elevated on the top of a mountain with a staff in my hand while a spotted jaguar charged at me. Then I touched its cheek with the staff and it fell down below my right side stationed.

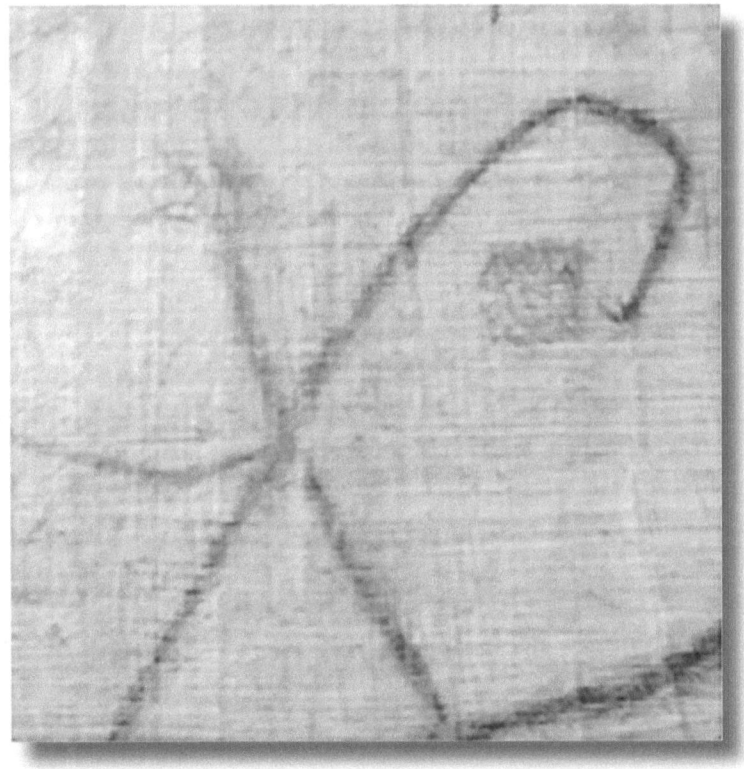

In November 2013, I dreamed that I was in the middle of a road and three men on black horses surrounded me, but they could not move. The horses were shaken by the light from the sky. I remained steadfast at the center of the road. Then a voice sounded out, "She has freed a thousand slaves with her reciting of the Surah Al-Barqarah." The third horseman rode around until he went to the other side of the road, remaining some distance away. People began running and passing in front of me and around me in all directions looking into my eyes and forming a line in a straight path on the road. Many years earlier, I remember seeing deceased family members in a line waiting for me. My dad was in front of the line at a gate. Questioned by the gatekeeper, "Why are you here?" he stated, "To enter the House of Stephanie." My father was instructed to perform a "wudu" (cleansing with water for purification) upon entering. Also, the next week, I had encounters with my ancestors showing me land and mathematical equations written on sand. The man with a long robe, with a turban on his head, and small staff in his hand was also showing me symbols. During the second visit, he directed me to look in the sky. I saw the letter Z, and then the third visit consisted of algorithm equations. I did not understand the meaning at first. Then shortly after, I saw myself traveling on a donkey and people were looking for me. I just returned from helping some women with traditional medicine. I was surprised to meet some family members looking for me to get a part of a book that was with me. I asked them to wait patiently on my return, but they left quickly without even an utterance of a word. All of this may seem a bit strange. However, my journey was predestined for greater works in my earthly life. Then my father appeared in a large house with a large hammer in his hand. He had killed two large snakes coming through a window. Later in the week, I saw myself lying in a basket while two brothers were tending and grooming horses in a stable. An old woman joined them and said, "The baby needs to know her identity." They agreed, but a younger woman approached them and said no. Waking up, I felt that something was going on and I put my trust in the Creator. I fell back to sleep and had another dream where I was greeted by a sheik and his two daughters asking for lodging. I welcomed them and shortly after, I found myself performing my *umrah* with my camel and rope, to tie her while I entered sacred ground. I enter the Ka'aba to perform my prayer. On January 18, 2014, in my dream, I saw a group of people standing out in front of a masjid and family members present looking at a bright star, and then an eagle started circling. People began asking for a blessing and then an eagle flew over me across my left side. It landed in front of my feet and bowed down raising his head up and looked into my eyes. Ten days later in my dream, I was lifted into the sky from the top of the bridge, surrounded by water, and I was traveling through darkness and with the light in my right index finger pointing out proclaiming Allah's name, "La ilaha illa'llah" (there is no God but God). I reached a door with a lock on it and it was broken, and then two little children ran out and I opened another door walking, and the lock was broken and more children came out. They followed me out into the light, and a woman was standing in the road and was thrown out of the path when I was reciting "Allah is one!" Next, I encountered an African man with a tambourine in his hand, shaking it and blocking a passageway. I proceeded and he moved out of the way, and then I entered with the little children. An unidentified Caucasian male stated, "She has freed them." Also across the left side, another Caucasian male, standing near an open gate, shouted, "My brand is on them. They belong to me." I responded, "No, they do not. They belong to Allah and no one else."

Two days later, on January 20, 2014, I dreamed I was standing next to a large hut-style house on the mountain surrounded by water. The earth began to move, and people were falling down all around me. I heard a woman's voice shout out, "Take care of my baby." I began looking startled and then a man dressed in a sailor suit said, "I have her money." Then I was taken away to school and given a pair of shoes, with the left looking different from the right. Then the teacher said, "I have something for you." I responded by saying, "I want my father," then my father appeared. He said, "you can reach me any time you call." So my father continued to tell me that he has a supplement for me since I was a little girl and was always ill, but a lady is hiding it and does not want to give it to him.

Afterwards, my father began speaking with a man with a turban on his head and said, "Is my daughter's name in the book?" The man said, "What is your daughter's name?" My father said, "I will call her and she will tell you." So, he dialed me on his phone and he said, "Tell the man your name," and I said, "Stephanie." And he said, "No! What is your name?" I said, "Safinat," and he said, "Haja." Then the man said, "Oh, sir, she is our daughter," and then my dad said, "Yes, she is. Write her name first in the book." And he began writing my name first in the book at the top on the right. Prior to February 22, 2014, my vision was seeing myself joined with women seated in gold seats with pearls and rubies encrusted on iron. It was a beautiful sight, waiting to enter a large white dome-shaped masjid similar to the Masjid Jami. I did my prayer at 11:11 a.m. with an intention to take a pilgrimage to the Iberian Peninsula.

All praises and glory belong to Allah. My journey has ended with seven stages of my earthly task. I relate my visions to my ancestors reaching me through divine intervention by Allah's will. First stage: *Victory*, over my enemy. Second stage: *Elevation*, meaning beloved by the creator. Third stage: *Garden*, which suggests the enrichment of life. Fourth stage: *Mountain*, which represents having a high status. Fifth stage: *Rope*. In a dream, this represents a binding agreement. Sixth stage: *Door or Gate*, represents a new beginning. Seventh stage: *Keys*, which means to unlock the truth on the path to knowledge. All of the above is true. Maybe my path is out of the ordinary and hard for most to understand, but my ancestors have reached me and remained with me in spirit throughout my walk to freedom and redemption. I prayed for normal sleep for myself and rest for my ancestors. See, I would always pray for the world to be healed and to be at peace. Finally, on August 8, 2015, my prayers were answered. I could not believe my vision showed my ancestors in regalia, stomping with joy, not like the terrible experiences most of them encountered during the epic "*Trail of Tears*." I then knew I did what was expected of me during these ten long years of searching for answers to many unknown questions. All praises to the one and only Great Spirit who takes care of all of mankind and every living organism. I hope my spiritual journey can offer any lost soul a purpose to keep believing in a higher power. Yes! Miracles are real and destiny is ordained by the Creator's will. I knew all my life I was different than most. For sure, seeing dead people is not part of a daily activity for humans on this earth. Or is it? Regardless, my life is filled with strange phenomena. We know scientists have found cases that were hard to explain, maybe even contradictory. For that purpose, let's just take a look down memory lane. I'm a descendant of a secret clan of Indians with chieftaincy. Since my youth my ancestors have always appeared to me, but it was not until I gained enough wisdom to truly understand why their life experiences were revealed to me. Prior to my enlightenment in 1982, I was haunted by a black crow who touched the crown of my head, its feet were entangled in my hair, and one of my peers tried to help get the bird off. The traumatic experience happened at Lamar University in Beaumont, Texas years ago. Everything in life happens for a reason, I was the little girl with a gift of sight, chosen to tell the story of my ancestor's path to freedom. After witnessing both past and future issues that remain among our people, I decided to continue my advocacy work on behalf of underrepresented communities, by furthering my education. Recently, I was blessed and honored to assume a role as council member for the Atakapa-Ishak Nation. My Atakapa ancestors have lived in Louisiana and Texas for centuries. Both states are known for having refineries producing large barrels of oil per day. Consequently, many of my families, including myself and other residents, have been exposed to the dangerous elements affecting their environment. Moreover, the effects of the chemicals from the refineries have polluted the air and water quality for all people, especially the Native American families who still live on tribal land. Our people are at the mercy of big corporations. This injustice is spawned into a new face of genocide to a nation of people who are the pillars of their society. I'm a humanitarian and my tears are of infinite numbers.

Now, I come forward to speak for many that have no voice but like the eagle in flight preparing to capture his prey, its cry will be heard. As human beings, we forget to care for others because we can be easily distracted in our own self-indulgence.

I am the little girl who has faced many barriers in life who has found favor with her Creator. I'm from the house of Paul Isaac, John Joseph, Sylvester Red Bud, and Adeline Brown. Anajatjaguar, who climbed trees, ate mud pies, and played freely on ancestral land as a child often communicated with deceased family members. My ancestral lineage is dated far back to kings and queens, bearing children to continue our heritage through wandering in the deserts across the oceans to the New World to be named chiefs and Indian shamans.

I'm the daughter of the Nation of Ishak! We are the keepers of the Holy Book, as my great-uncle declared. We are those ancient Indians who hunted prehistoric animals and lived in harmony with Mother Nature. My blood origin through DNA markers represents Neolithic migration in the Americas and my ancestors were a part of the agriculture evolution.

These Afro-Asiatic tribes of the Atakapan Indian Groups the Bidai and Akokisas were some of my ancestors who first had contact with the Europeans. Our heritage has been clouded with different spellings throughout history (Atacapas, Atakapans, Atakapas, also known as the infamous Choctaw slur called "man eaters". During the Cabeza de Vaca expedition in the 1500s, he called the people the "Han People. Our DNA reveals who we are. I know that to be a fact because I've always had spiritual encounters through vision with my ancestors.

Pictured are the children of Christ the King Mission in Louisiana.

My Muslim name is Safinat and it is derived from the word "Zakah," which literally means growth, blessings, purification, and or praises. The ship to salvation, the transporter of the desert, derived from the Syrian word "Akkare," meaning farmers. I was the ship that carried my ancestor's stories letting their voices be heard.

My journey ends!

Resources

Special thanks to the Special Collections and University Archives department at Marquette University.

Lotus flower retrieved from https://pixabay.com/en/lotus-flower-summer-zen-lake-978659/

p. 2 (Hosea 4:6)

p. 9 retrieved from Ancestry.com

p. 10-11 Thibodeaux, G. (1999) On the Banks of Plaquemine Brulée. Une Histoire de la Pointe de l'Eglise Church Point, Louisiana. microfilm: 2340555]

p. 44, Image of Women retrieved from https://pixabay.com/en/woman-african-black-female-ethnic-241979/

p. 44, Conrad, G. (1990) The Attakapas Doomsday Book: Land Grants, Claims, & Confirmations in the Attakapas District.

p. 45 Webster, J., Boahen, A., & Idowu, H. (1967). Growth of African Civilisation: The Revolutionary Years West Africa since 1800. p.137

p. 46 O'Neil, D. (n.d.). Distribution of Bloodtypes. Retrieved from http://anthro.palomar.edu/vary/vary 3.htm

p. 46, A dictionary of the Atakapa language accompanied by text material, by Albert S. Gatschet and John R. Swanton (1932)

p. 47 Jolivette, A. (2003) Creole diaspora: (Re)articulating the social, legal, economic, and regional construction of American Indian identity. University of California Santa Cruz.[Dissertation] p.5

p. 48 (Exodus 3:8).

p. 48-49, Besson, E. (2014). SE Texas' Atakapa tribe seeking federal designation. Beaumont Enterprise & Journal[Interview with chief of the Atakapa Tribe]

p. 49, (Personal Communication) Chief Michael Amos

p. 50 (Interview) Smith, M. (2007) Atakapa says culture still alive. History and Wildlife. Retrieved from https://w w w.i nd i a nc ou nt r y ne w s .c om /i nde x .php /ne w s /history-wildlife/1455-atakapas-say-culture-still-alive

p. 84, Image of Jaguar retrieved from https://pixabay.com/en/ animal-carnivore-cat-dangerous-21478/

p. 91, Special Collections and University Archives, Raynor MemorialUniversity, Marquette University. [Image of Children at Christ the King Mission in Louisiana]

Stephanie Colligan-Ishola, *Biography*
Pronouns (she, her, hers)

She has a master's in Clinical Mental Health and is a sexual assault advocate with the Attorney General's Office in the State of Texas. Stephanie is an international registered Mental Health Facilitator, CASA Guardian Ad-Litem, & Certified Crisis Instructor. Her humanitarian and advocacy work began 30 years ago and continues to this day. Her passion for researching and collaborating with local officials, organizations, stakeholders, and community members to empower those in need, can be seen through her various activities promoting social change among marginalized communities.

She is a lifetime member of the American Federation of Teachers, a recent member of the American Counseling Association, Chi Sigma Iota International Professional Honor Society, National Society of Leadership & Success, American Psychological Association Campus Ambassador, member of the National Organization for Human Services, National Society of Collegiate Scholars, The Society of Collegiate Leadership & Achievement, and volunteer for the Medical Reserve Corps. She received recognition from Harris County Commissioner Rodney Ellis for her empowering at-risk communities and an award from Parents and Public Schools for her dedication to youth and the President's Volunteer Award at the Gold Level for commitment to strengthen our nations and communities through volunteer service.

www.ingramcontent.com/pod-product-compliance
Lightning Source LLC
Chambersburg PA
CBHW020329130626
46549CB00003B/1096